The
Princeton
Review®

ASAP
Human
Geography

By the Staff of The Princeton Review

princetonreview.com

Penguin
Random
House

The Princeton Review
110 East 42nd St, 7th Floor
New York, NY 10017
editorialsupport@review.com

Published in the United States by Penguin
Random House LLC, New York, and in Canada
by Random House of Canada, a division of
Penguin Random House Ltd., Toronto.

ISBN: 978-1-5247-5765-6
eBook ISBN: 978-1-5247-5770-0
ISSN: 2574-1187

AP and Advanced Placement are registered
trademarks of the College Board, which is not
affiliated with The Princeton Review.

The Princeton Review is not affiliated with
Princeton University.

Editor: Selena Coppock
Production Editors: Emily Epstein White and
                   Melissa Duclos
Production Artists: Deborah A. Silvestrini and
                   Craig Patches

Printed in the United States of America.

10 9 8 7 6 5 4 3 2 1

Editorial

Rob Franek, Editor-in-Chief
Casey Cornelius, VP Content Development
Mary Beth Garrick, Director of Production
Selena Coppock, Managing Editor
Meave Shelton, Senior Editor
Colleen Day, Editor
Sarah Litt, Editor
Aaron Riccio, Editor
Orion McBean, Associate Editor

Penguin Random House Publishing Team

Tom Russell, VP, Publisher
Alison Stoltzfus, Publishing Director
Jake Eldred, Associate Managing Editor
Ellen Reed, Production Manager
Suzanne Lee, Designer

Acknowledgments

The editor of this book would like to thank the tremendous content development team: Eliz Markowitz, Briana Gordon, Jason Morgan, and Matt Gironda. When I put out the call for content creators willing to take on a project that was little more than a loose brainstorm, you all gladly jumped without a net and delivered brilliant ideas, charts, and visual concepts. Thank you so much for your hard work, enthusiasm, and Human Geo humor.

The reason that this brand-new series looks so gorgeous is because Debbie Silvestrini and Craig Patches are on the case. Your unending dedication, hard work, and imagination have made working on this series an absolute pleasure. Is there anything cooler than asking for a smiley face icon and getting one who is wearing sunglasses?

Contents

Get More (Free) Content

1 Go to **PrincetonReview.com/cracking.**

2 Enter the following ISBN for your book: 9781524757656.

3 Answer a few simple questions to set up an exclusive Princeton Review account. (If you already have one, you can just log in.)

4 Click the "Student Tools" button, also found under "My Account" from the top toolbar. You're all set to access your bonus content!

Need to report a potential **content** issue?

Contact **EditorialSupport@review.com.**
Include:

- full title of the book
- ISBN number
- page number

Need to report a **technical** issue?

Contact **TPRStudentTech@review.com**
and provide:

- your full name
- email address used to register the book
- full book title and ISBN
- computer OS (Mac/PC) and browser (Firefox, Safari, etc.)

Once you've registered, you can...

- Get valuable advice about the college application process, including tips for writing a great essay and where to apply for financial aid

- If you're still choosing between colleges, use our searchable rankings of *The Best 382 Colleges* to find out more information about your dream school

- Check to see if there have been any corrections or updates to this edition

- Get our take on any recent or pending updates to the AP Human Geography Exam

Introduction

What Is This Book and When Should I Use It?

Welcome to *ASAP Human Geography*, your quick-review study guide for the AP Human Geography Exam written by the Staff of The Princeton Review. This is a brand-new series custom built for crammers, visual learners, and any student doing high-level AP concept review. As you read through this book, you will notice that there aren't any practice tests, end-of-chapter drills, or multiple-choice questions. There's also very little test-taking strategy presented in here. Both of those things (practice and strategy) can be found in The Princeton Review's other top-notch AP series—*Cracking*. So if you need a deep dive into AP Human Geography, check out *Cracking the AP Human Geography Exam* at your local bookstore.

ASAP Human Geography is our fast track to understanding the material—like a fantastic set of class notes. We present the most important information that you MUST know (or should know or could know—more on that later) in visually friendly formats such as charts, graphs, and maps, and we even threw a few jokes in there to keep things interesting.

Use this book anytime you want—it's never too late to do some studying (or is it ever too early). It's small, so you can take it with you anywhere and crack it open while you're waiting for soccer practice to start or for your friend to meet you for a study date or for the library to open*. *ASAP Human Geography* is the perfect study guide for students who need high-level review in addition to their regular review and also for students who perhaps need to cram pre-exam. Whatever you need it for, you'll find no judgment here!

---

*Because you camp out in front of it like they are selling concert tickets in there, right? Only kidding.

Who Is This Book For?

This book is for YOU! No matter what kind of student you are, this book is the right one for you. How do you know what kind of student you are? Follow this handy chart to find out!

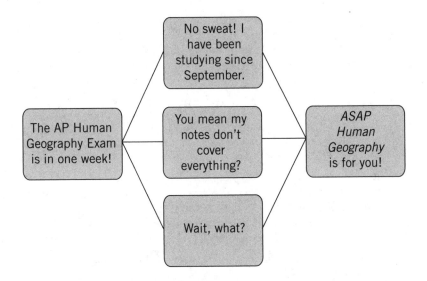

As you can see, this book is meant for every kind of student. Our quick lessons let you focus on the topics you must know, you should know, and you could know—that way, even if the test is tomorrow (!), you can get a little extra study time in, and only learn the material you need.

How Do I Use This Book?

This book is your study tool, so feel free to customize it in whatever way makes the most sense to you, given your available time to prepare. Here are some suggestions:

Target Practice

If you know what topics give you the most trouble, hone in on those chapters or sections.

ASK Away

Answer all of the ASK questions *first*. This will help you to identify any additional tough spots that may need special attention.

Three-Pass System

Start at the very beginning!* Read the book several times from cover to cover, focusing selectively on the MUST content for your first pass, the SHOULD content for your second pass, and finally, the COULD content.

 *It's a very good place to start.

Why Are There Icons?

Your standard AP course is designed to be equivalent to a college-level class, and as such, the amount of material that's covered may seem overwhelming. It's certainly admirable to want to learn everything—these are, after all, fascinating subjects. But every student's course load, to say nothing of his or her life, is different, and there isn't always time to memorize every last fact.

To that end, *ASAP Human Geography* doesn't just distill the key information into bite-sized chunks and memorable tables and figures. This book also breaks down the material into three major types of content:

 This symbol calls out a section that has MUST KNOW information. This is the core content that is either the most likely to appear in some format on the test or is foundational knowledge that's needed to make sense of other highly tested topics.

This symbol refers to SHOULD KNOW material. This is either content that has been tested in some form before (but not as frequently) or which will help you to deepen your understanding of the surrounding topics. If you're pressed for time, you might just want to skim it, and read only those sections that you feel particularly unfamiliar with.

This symbol indicates COULD KNOW material, but don't just write it off! This material is still within the AP's expansive curriculum, so if you're aiming for a perfect 5, you'll still want to know all of this. That said, this is the information that is least likely to be directly tested, so if the test is just around the corner, you should probably save this material for last.

As you work through the book, you'll also notice a few other types of icons.

 The Ask Yourself question is an opportunity to solidify your understanding of the material you've just read. It's also a great way to take these concepts outside of the book and make the sort of real-world connections that you'll need in order to answer the free-response questions on the AP Exam.

 The Remember symbol indicates certain facts that you should keep in mind as you're going through the different sections.

 There's a reason why people still say that "All work and no play" is a bad thing. These jokes help to shake your brain up a bit and keep it from just glazing over all of the content—they're a bit like mental speed bumps, there to keep you from going too fast for your own good.

 There's a lot to think about in this book, and when you see this guy (the Did You Know? icon), you know that the information that follows is always good to have on hand. You'll rock it in trivia, if no place else.

Where Can I Find Other Resources?

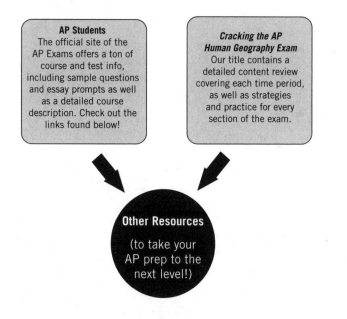

AP Students
The official site of the AP Exams offers a ton of course and test info, including sample questions and essay prompts as well as a detailed course description. Check out the links found below!

Cracking the AP Human Geography Exam
Our title contains a detailed content review covering each time period, as well as strategies and practice for every section of the exam.

Other Resources
(to take your AP prep to the next level!)

Useful Links

- AP Students Homepage: https://apstudent.collegeboard.org.
- AP Human Geography Homepage: www.apstudent.collegeboard.org/apcourse/ap-human-geography
- Your Student Tools: www.PrincetonReview.com/cracking
  See the "Register Your Book Online!" page for step-by-step instructions for registering your book and accessing more materials to boost your test prep.

CHAPTER 1

Geography: Its Nature and Perspectives

In this chapter we will review the central concepts, skills, and tools in human geography that may show up on the AP Human Geography exam. This includes knowledge of notable geographers and their key contributions and geographical models. We will also review the essentials of maps, map types, map scale, and landscape analysis.

Geography as a Field of Inquiry !!

Geography is something we all study and practice, whether we are aware of it or not. Every individual has a personal geographical understanding of the world through which he or she forms a global perspective.

People in a wide variety of fields are beginning to use these geographic perspectives to analyze and solve significant problems facing our world. AP Human Geography focuses on exactly this: approaching the study of geography through an analytic perspective. Understanding geographical models, concepts, and tools facilitates the advancement of geography as a field of inquiry.

Evolution of Key Geographical Concepts !!

Populations, land, and political boundaries are constantly evolving, and so are the ways in which we observe, understand, and predict them. Let's examine some key concepts and formulas used to quantify these geographical changes.

Natural Population Increase 💬

By comparing the birth rate and death rate for a country, we can calculate the **rate of natural increase (RNI)**. If you subtract the death rate from the birth rate, the difference is the amount of population change per thousand members of the population for that year. Divide the result by 10 to calculate the RNI. The RNI is also the annual percentage of population growth of that country for that one-year period. Make sure to put a % sign after you get the answer to the equation.

$$RNI = \frac{Birth\ Rate - Death\ Rate}{10}$$

In rare situations, it is possible to have a negative RNI. Mathematically, the death rate can be larger than the birth rate, resulting in a negative number that is divided by 10 to get the negative RNI. When the RNI is negative, it means the population has shrunk during the year the data was collected.

Germany is a prime example where the already low birth rates have dipped below death rates and as a result the RNI has ranged between −0.1% and −0.2%, annually. For more examples, look at the stage one and stage four parts of the Demographic Transition Model in found in Chapters 2, 5, 6 (we just can't get enough of that model).

Why "Natural Increase?

RNI does not account for **immigration** or **emigration**—people arriving in the country or exiting the country. A nation with a high rate of natural increase can have an unexpectedly low long-term population prediction if there is a large amount of emigration. Conversely, a country with a low rate of natural increase can still grow significantly over time if the number of immigrants is high.

Population Doubling Time 🔊

We can try to quickly estimate how long it would take for a country to double in size by this formula:

$$\text{Doubling Time} = \frac{70}{\text{Rate of Natural Increase}}\text{*}$$

Example: An RNI of 1.9% in Bolivia would result in a doubling time of 36.8 years. That's fast, but unless something changes significantly in Bolivian society, we expect the 10 million people of today to grow to 20 million by 2050. But it won't. Why not? There is negative net migration in Bolivia. Out-migration to other countries reduces the long-term prediction to around 17 million by 2050. This is why we call the RNI an estimate.

The more accurate way would be to estimate the RNI for each year in the future by examining a country's position on the **Demographic Transition Model.** Then you would multiply each year's population by the RNI and add that to the next year's growth, and so on, and so on:

$$(\text{Pop.} \times \text{RNI}_1) \times \text{RNI}_2 \times \text{RNI}_3 \times \dots \times \text{RNI}_n = \text{Future Population}$$

Rank-Size Rule for Cities 🔊

Population geographers have recognized an urban hierarchy of city populations, especially in countries with long social histories. The **rank-size rule** is a commonly observed statistical relationship between the population sizes and population ranks of a nation's cities. Under the rank-size rule, a country's second largest city is half the size of its largest city; the third-largest city is one-third the size of the largest city; and so on, such that the eighth largest city is one-eighth the size of the largest city.

---

 *Other types of doubles that you won't need to know for the exam: tennis, Dutch, trouble, Stuffed Oreos, mint gum, Jeopardy Daily, Cheeseburger.

Here's the rank-size rule as a formula:

The nth largest city is $\frac{1}{n}$ the size of the country's largest city

While few countries have city populations that precisely follow the rule, the hierarchy of cities in the United States or in Russia is a close approximation of the rule.

Distance-Decay Functions ❗

The effect of distance on relationships is important to understand, and geographers often utilize the concept of **distance decay** to explain **relative distance**. Distance decay means that the farther away different places are from a place of origin, the less likely interaction will be with the original place.

Relative distance is also expressed by the principle of **Tobler's law**, which states that all places are interrelated, but closer places are more related than farther ones. Does that sound confusing to you? Let's dig into this a bit on the next page.

Tobler's law (1970) states that all places are interrelated, but closer places are more related than farther ones. American-Swiss geographer and cartographer Waldo Tobler recognized that when the length of distance becomes a factor that inhibits the interaction between two points, this is known as the **friction of distance**. This can be seen when the combined time and cost of moving a product prevents it from being sold in far-off locations. Let's see this in a situation that you might see this evening.

Tobler's Law of Dinner

You know you should eat a healthy dinner, but that would mean braving the 10-minute journey to the grocery store and buying vegetables for a few bucks, then heading to your kitchen to cook up the vegetables— perhaps in some oil, with salt and pepper. So you really won't be eating your healthy dinner for 45 minutes or so. Why bother when you already have a pizza in the freezer? With just a few, FREE steps and the push of a button, dinner is served.

Notable Geographers and their Models ❗

Land use, or how property is utilized, shared, or divided can say a lot about culture through its imprint on the landscape. Let's learn about some land use models developed by some notable geographers throughout history.

Geographer	Model	Year	Central Tenet
Johan Heinrich von Thünen	The Isolated State Model	1826	Crops or animals that require lots of attention are going to be closest to the town, and the ones that require the least attention will be farthest
Larry Ford and Ernest Griffin	Latin American City Model	1980	Depicts the common urban landscapes of international locations
Alfred Weber	Theory of Industrial Location	1909	The selection of optimal factory locations has much to do with the minimization of land, labor, resource, and transportation costs
Walter Christaller	Central Place Theory	1920s	There is a hierarchy of places (seven levels, from a small hamlet to the large regional service-center city) across the landscape that follows a regular pattern

Von Thünen's Land Use Model ❗

You're very likely to see a reference to von Thünen's Land Use Model on the AP Human Geography Exam. Here's a handy chart explaining each section of land use found in that model.

von Thünen's Lane Use Model
also known as The Isolated State Model

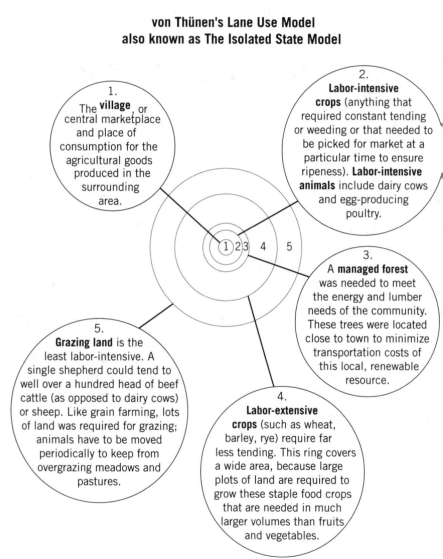

1.
The **village** or central marketplace and place of consumption for the agricultural goods produced in the surrounding area.

2.
Labor-intensive crops (anything that required constant tending or weeding or that needed to be picked for market at a particular time to ensure ripeness). **Labor-intensive animals** include dairy cows and egg-producing poultry.

3.
A **managed forest** was needed to meet the energy and lumber needs of the community. These trees were located close to town to minimize transportation costs of this local, renewable resource.

4.
Labor-extensive crops (such as wheat, barley, rye) require far less tending. This ring covers a wide area, because large plots of land are required to grow these staple food crops that are needed in much larger volumes than fruits and vegetables.

5.
Grazing land is the least labor-intensive. A single shepherd could tend to well over a hundred head of beef cattle (as opposed to dairy cows) or sheep. Like grain farming, lots of land was required for grazing; animals have to be moved periodically to keep from overgrazing meadows and pastures.

Did You Know?

Central Business District

In the Latin American City model, the Central Business District (CBD) is located at the center of the model. All cities possess a CBD—it's an area with the highest density of commercial land use. In your area, you may think of this area as "downtown." In Latin American cities, historically, the Laws of the Indies stipulated that each settlement have a central square known as a plaza. This was to reproduce the style of European cities such as Madrid, which has at its center the Plaza de Mayor. Surrounding the plaza, the centers of government, religion, and commerce are located. Today, the CBD remains the primary location for businesses.

This is unlike the United States and Canada, where numerous suburban CBDs dominate the economy.

CBDs in Latin America are also vertically oriented and most large cities have a cluster of skyscrapers at their core. Turn the page to feast your eyes on a Latin American Land Use Model.

This model is important as an example of the colonial city. The effects of European colonial rule on many cities in Latin America, Africa, and Asia are significant. Often colonial powers demolished old pre-colonial cities and rebuilt them in the European style. In other cases, new cities were built according to specific plans. The Latin American model tends to represent the latter. During the 1500s, the Spanish government in the New World enacted a number of colonial legal codes collectively known as the **Laws of the Indies.** One of these laws dealt specifically with the planning and the layout of colonial cities.

The Latin American City Model

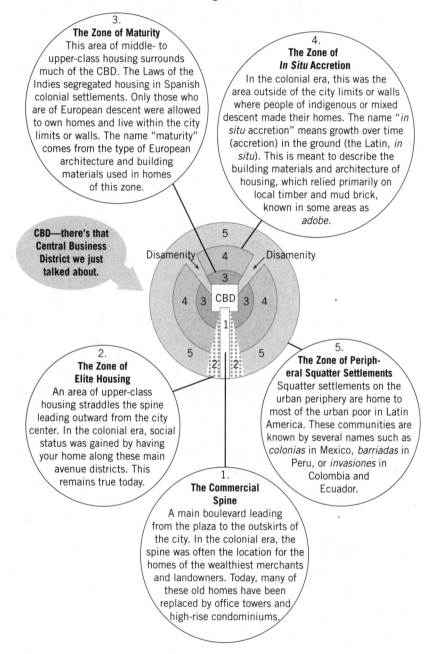

3.
The Zone of Maturity
This area of middle- to upper-class housing surrounds much of the CBD. The Laws of the Indies segregated housing in Spanish colonial settlements. Only those who are of European descent were allowed to own homes and live within the city limits or walls. The name "maturity" comes from the type of European architecture and building materials used in homes of this zone.

4.
The Zone of *In Situ* Accretion
In the colonial era, this was the area outside of the city limits or walls where people of indigenous or mixed descent made their homes. The name "*in situ* accretion" means growth over time (accretion) in the ground (the Latin, *in situ*). This is meant to describe the building materials and architecture of housing, which relied primarily on local timber and mud brick, known in some areas as *adobe*.

CBD—there's that Central Business District we just talked about.

Disamenity

Disamenity

2.
The Zone of Elite Housing
An area of upper-class housing straddles the spine leading outward from the city center. In the colonial era, social status was gained by having your home along these main avenue districts. This remains true today.

5.
The Zone of Peripheral Squatter Settlements
Squatter settlements on the urban periphery are home to most of the urban poor in Latin America. These communities are known by several names such as *colonias* in Mexico, *barriadas* in Peru, or *invasiones* in Colombia and Ecuador.

1.
The Commercial Spine
A main boulevard leading from the plaza to the outskirts of the city. In the colonial era, the spine was often the location for the homes of the wealthiest merchants and landowners. Today, many of these old homes have been replaced by office towers and high-rise condominiums.

The Weber Model: Industrial Location Theory ❗

The location of factories has been the focus of much economic and geographic study. Going back to the work of **Alfred Weber**, whose 1909 *Theory of Industrial Location* is still influential, the selection of optimal factory locations has much to do with the minimization of land, labor, resource, and transportation costs. By their nature, manufactured goods have a variable-cost framework that affects the potential location of factory sites. Weber states that in terms of location, manufactured goods can be classified into two categories based on the amount of inputs in relation to product output:

Weight-gaining or bulk-gaining manufacturing: inputs that are combined to make a final product that gains bulk, volume, or weight in production process. These factories tend to be located closer to consumers because the cost of transporting the finished product is more than the cost of transporting the inputs (ex: refrigerators, cars).

Weight-losing or bulk-reducing manufacturing: large number of inputs that are reduced to a final product that weighs less or has less volume/bulk than the inputs. These factories tend to be located near the inputs that lose the most bulk in the manufacturing process (ex: trees, metal ore).

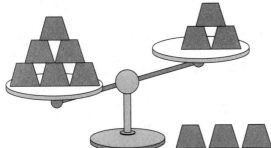

 Ask Yourself...

Can you think of specific cities or towns that you're familiar with that are examples of weight-gaining/bulk-gaining manufacturing and weight-losing/bulk-reducing manufacturing?

Christaller's Central Place Theory ❶

Central place theory holds that all market areas are focused on a central settlement that is a place of exchange and service provision.

The **market areas** of settlements (also called **hinterlands**) overlap one another at different scales. Large settlements have larger market areas, but they are few in number, whereas small settlements have smaller, more numerous market areas. In terms of the size of market areas, large settlements have a larger number of services, for which consumers are willing to travel large distances to access. Small settlements have a smaller number of services, which are closer to consumers.

Large settlements:

- Large market areas, but they are few in number
- Larger number of services for which consumers are willing to travel far
- Example: Ikea—it's a bit of a drive, but they have EVERYTHING. Maybe you'll visit once or twice a year.

Small settlements:

- Small market areas but many of them
- Small number of services that are close to consumers
- Example: Target furniture section—it's around the corner, has all the basics, and you visit often—sometimes by accident!

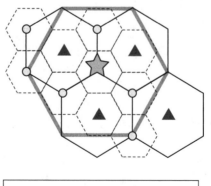

o Village	--- Village Market Area
▲ Town	— Town Market Area
⭐ City	▬ City Market Area

Research in the 1920s by German theorist **Walter Christaller** showed that there is a hierarchy of places (seven levels, from a small hamlet to the large regional service-center city) across the landscape that followed a regular pattern. Christaller used hexagons to represent individual market areas. (See that nifty image on page 12.) Then, he overlapped smaller-scale patterns with larger scale layers of hexagonal market areas. That diagram is a cutaway of three layers of this **urban hierarchy** as a basic example of Christaller's theoretical principles. In this example, the city's market area (or hinterland) contains three towns and five villages. One village and one town lie outside the city's market area.

Try an Example...

Use food stores to understand this principle. Break it down this way:

- A village is like a convenience shop (such as 7-Eleven, Circle K, Wawa, Tedeschi Food Shops, Duane Reade)

- A town is like a grocery (such as Safeway, Kroger, Stop & Shop, Albertsons)

- A city is like a big box warehouse store (Sam's Cub, BJ's, Costco).

People are willing to travel different distances for the service of food retailing. These market areas are based on the number of goods available in the store and the volume discount received when purchasing in bulk.

Need a bottle of soda?

Just go to the local convenience store for a 20-ounce bottle for $1.29. Head further to a grocery store, if you desire a 2-liter bottle for $1.09. And go all the way to the big-box warehouse store if you want a case of 24 20-ounce bottles for $17.00.

 Ask Yourself...

Brainstorm some other parallels for the village/town/city structure that we discuss above. What other types of things have a similar type of formal structure? Drawing parallels is crucial for solid essay writing, so brainstorm some ideas and remember, no idea is too offbeat!

Concepts Underlying Geographical Perspective

Each person's geographical perspective is unique, but concepts under-lying this perspective encompass six main areas that you must know for the AP exam: scale, location, space, place, and pattern.

Scale

Map Scale

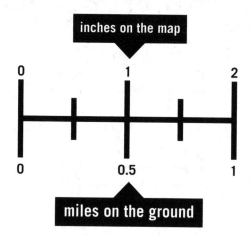

Relative Scale

National

Regional

Local

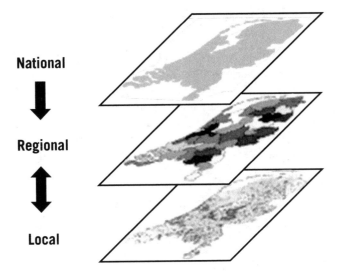

Scale is the relationship of an object or place to the Earth as a whole. Scale can be thought about two ways in geography:

1. **Map scale:** the ratio of distance on a map and distance in the real world in absolute terms.

2. **Relative scale**, or what can also be referred to as the **scale of analysis**. This describes the **level of aggregation**, or in other words, the level at which you group things together for examination. Relative scales can range from the individual or the local, from city to county and state, from regional to national to continental, or to the international and global scales.

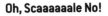

Oh, Scaaaaaale No!

Be careful not to compare different scales of analysis or places at different scales. For example, it would be wrong to just visit Atlanta and assume the rest of Georgia had the same characteristics as that one city. Likewise, if you examined economic data from Wyoming and assumed the rest of the United States had the same median income, types of businesses, or unemployment rates, you would be incorrect.

Did You Know?

Worth Its Weight In Points: Remember that free-response questions are carefully graded based on a metric. Specifying the scale of the items you're being asked about may earn you points for detail of example material. Specify whether a company is a transnational corporation or a local business or if you are discussing a local government, a federal regulation, or an international organization. Much of that information may be in your book, but may also be found in simply being a student of history and culture, so flip through the newspaper or read a historical nonfiction book for pleasure. ABL—Always Be Learnin'!

[Please accept our immediate and sincere apologies for that super corny joke.]

Location 🛈

The concept of location, like scale, can be considered in relative and absolute terms.

1. **Absolute location** defines a point or place on the map using coordinates such as latitude and longitude.

2. **Relative location**, by contrast, refers to the location of a place compared to a known place or geographic feature.

Absolute Location ❗

Keeping latitude and longitude straight (pun intended)
- Lines of latitude measure distance, in degrees, north or south of the equator (latitude = <u>ladder</u>).
- Lines of longitude measure distance, in degrees, east or west of the Prime Meridian (longitude = how <u>long</u> the ladder is).

Prime Meridian ❗

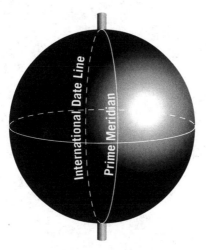

The Prime Meridian is 0° longitude. On the opposite side of the earth is the 180° line of longitude. Parts of this line compose the **International Date Line** that also meanders around a number of international boundaries.

Time Zones !

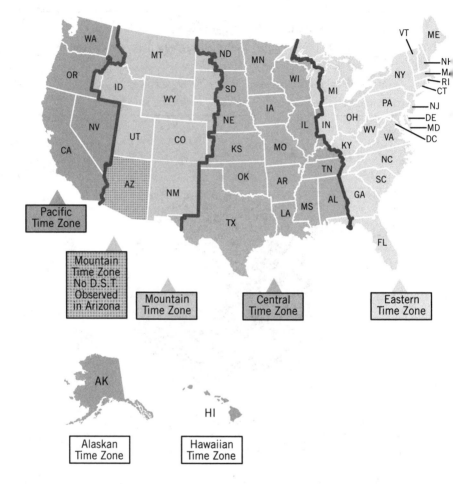

Time zones are divided up in 15-degree-wide longitudinal zones around the world (with some exceptions). This is because 360° divided by 24 hours a day equals 15°. One exception to this rule comes from China, where leaders established one time zone for the entire country. Another exception is North Korea, whose leaders decided in 2015 to create their very own spiffy time zone that is—get this—thirty minutes behind Japan and thirty minutes ahead of China. (Talk about a statement of political independence!) For practical purposes, dividing lines between time zones often follow political boundaries, sometimes even along local area divisions. Time zones were created relatively recently, in the era of transcontinental railways, to standardize time across long east-west train lines.

Relative Location

Relative location is based upon a place's relationship to other known geographic features or places. For instance, when people from Arlington, Virginia, are asked where they are from, they might say "Washington, D.C.," and people from Santa Monica, California, might say they are from Los Angeles, or simply L.A.

Did You Know?

Location, Location...Relative Location: Your relative location to a place can be highly valuable. In the early 1990s, Dublin, Ireland, became an important international business location due to its low-cost economy, English language skills, and close relative location to Great Britain, where the cost of doing business was extremely high (especially in London).

Space ❶

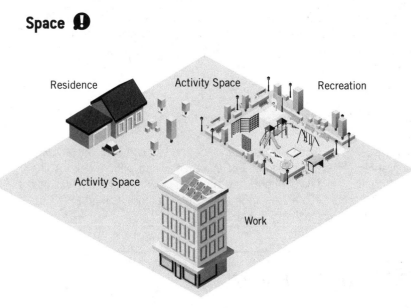

When geographers talk about **space**, they're not talking about "the final frontier" or anything outside of Earth's atmosphere. Instead, geographers are referring to the surface of the Earth. Geographical space is a bit of an abstract concept. Close your eyes and think of the global surface of the earth as an empty slate.

Imagine placing objects on the Earth's **spatial** surface that are defined by their location and are separated by some degree of distance from other things. These objects could be people, trees, buildings, or even whole cities—whatever you choose to visualize. So when geographers talk about **activity space** they're referring to an area wherein activity occurs on a daily basis. "Thinking spatially" means understanding the pattern and distribution of objects and analyzing their relationships, connectedness, movement, growth, and change across space and over time.

Two locational concepts that work together are **site** and **situation.** Site refers to the physical characteristics of a place, such as the fact that New York City is located on a large, deep water harbor, next to the Atlantic Ocean. **Situation** refers to the place's **interrelatedness** with other places. More on all of this later.

 Site and situation work together like peanut butter and jelly, like Tom and Jerry, like Abbi and Ilana.

Place ❗

Well, that was deep! The concept of **place** is less abstract, but still important theoretically. It's important to have an open and broad concept of place. Think of place as an area of bounded space of some human importance. People don't have to live there for it to be a place (think: desert or ocean).

Toponym

This is a fancy word for a place name assigned to a location when human importance is recognized. Place names often reveal the historical interrelatedness of location places.

Area of Bounded Space

Bounded sounds small right? Well, don't be deceived: an area of bounded space could be somewhere small, such as a room, or as large as a continent.

Types of Places

Places come in a huge variety: regions, urban places, places of work, resource locations, and transportation nodes, just to name a few. When considering the importance of a location, region, town, or city, it is necessary to consider: "Why does this place matter?"

Sequent Occupancy

The attributes of a place change over time. Sequent occupancy describes the succession (or evolution) of groups and cultural influences throughout a place's history.

Place-Specificity (Say that ten times fast!)

In many places we find that there are several different historical
layers that contribute to a **place:**
specific culture, society, local politics, and economy.

For example, the place specificity of Santa Fe, New Mexico, is a complex
mix of multiple Native American, Spanish colonial, and modern American
influences based upon the sequence of past and current societal
influences.

Pattern ❗

Now let's talk about how geographers use special terms to describe
different types of **spatial patterns;** we'll present that information in a
format that you might call a—wait for it—PATTERN.

Cluster
When things are grouped together on the earth's surface, the pattern is referred to as a cluster.

Agglomeration
When clustering occurs purposefully around a central point or an economic growth pole, it is referred to as agglomeration.

Sinuous
If it's wavy, the pattern is sinuous, like the graph of your heartbeat at the doctor's office.

Random
When there is no rhyme or reason to the distribution of a spatial phenomenon, it is referred to as a random pattern.

Scattered
Objects that are normally ordered, but appear dispersed, can be referred to as scattered.

Linear
If a pattern is in a straight line, it is linear.

Land survey patterns have an effect on the property lines and political boundaries of states and provinces. There are three main types of land survey patterns used in North America:

- East of central Ohio and Ontario, land surveys until the 1830s used natural landscape features to divide land on a system of **metes and bounds**, which had been developed in Europe centuries earlier.

- After the 1830s, when new techniques to accurately determine longitude were transferred from sea navigation to land survey, surveyors in the United States and Canada used a rectilinear **township and range** survey system based upon lines of latitude and longitude. This produced the block-shaped property lines and more geometric shape to many western states and provinces.

- Former French colonial areas such as Québec and Louisiana have **long-lot patterns**. These have a narrow frontage along a road or waterway with a very long lot shape behind.

Land Survey Patterns in North America

Metes and Bounds   Township and Range   Long lots

 Ask Yourself...

What are some more examples of cities or regions that showcase these land survey patterns? What are the pros and cons of each? Can you think of historical incidents or trends or movements that were helped or hurt by how that region's land is surveyed?

Diffusion Patterns ❗

There are a number of different ways and patterns in which human phenomena **diffuse** spatially or spread across the earth's surface. Most often we examine how culture, ideas, or technology spread from a point of origin to other parts of the world. Sometimes that point of origin or place of innovation is called a **hearth**. Here's a quick rundown of the different types of diffusion.

Type of Diffusion	Description	Example	
Hierarchical	Originates in a first-order location; moves down to second order locations; so on and so forth at increasingly local scales.	Spread of fashion trends from leaders/celebrities to ordinary citizens.	
Contagious	Moves outward from point of origin to nearby locations.	Communication of disease, or distribution of news in rural regions.	
Stimulus	Underlying principle diffuses, then stimulates creation of new products/ideas.	When gluten-free eating habits (principle) influence restaurants to offer more gluten-free dishes (new products).	
Expansion	Pattern expands outward from central origin in all directions.	The spread of spices from India to many other countries all over the world.	
Relocation	Begins at point of origin; crosses significant physical barrier; relocates on other side.	A population crossing a large mountain range and making its home on the other side.	

Using Landscape Analysis to Examine the Human Organization of Space 🔊

Humans and the land we live on are interconnected in a wide variety of ways. The AP Human Geography test will ask you about specific concepts surrounding the human-environment relationships and place-place relationships.

Human-Environment Relationships 🔊

The term **human-environment relationships**, or **human ecology**, is used to describe human interactions with nature. This includes farming practices, forestry techniques, fisheries, and environmental regulation.

Our ecological relationship to the land can be conceived of as a **food web** in which each type of crop and animal is dependent on a number of human inputs, soil and climate conditions, and other crops.

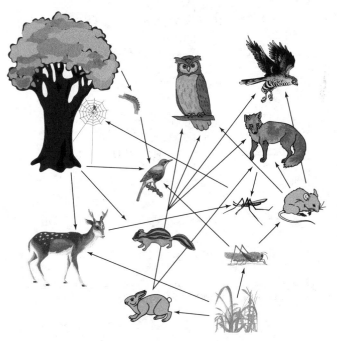

The term **food chain** can be used to detail the order of predators in the animal world.

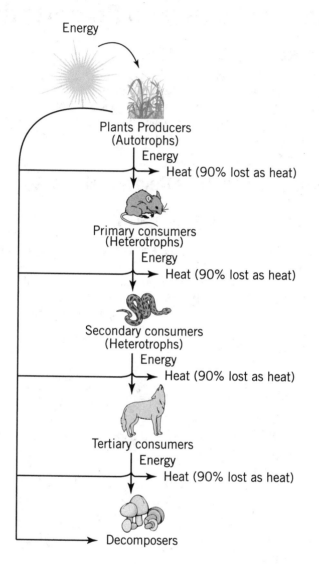

Energy

Plants Producers
(Autotrophs)
Energy
Heat (90% lost as heat)

Primary consumers
(Heterotrophs)
Energy
Heat (90% lost as heat)

Secondary consumers
(Heterotrophs)
Energy
Heat (90% lost as heat)

Tertiary consumers
Energy
Heat (90% lost as heat)

Decomposers

Some food chains you will NOT see on the test? Taco Bell, Ruby Tuesday, Applebee's, Subway, Pizza Hut, Starbucks…but feel free to study AT any of these.

In a more modern sense, **food chain** can also describe several integrated human and mechanical inputs, from developing seeds to planting, fertilizing, harvesting, processing, packaging, and transporting food to market...all the way to your dinner plate.

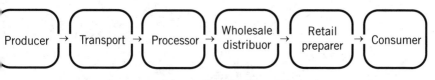

Producer → Transport → Processor → Wholesale distribuor → Retail preparer → Consumer

Segments of the modern-day food chain

 Did You Know?

Much of what you need to know for the Human-Environment Relationships portion
of the exam has to do with specific farming practices, so don't
skip this section!

Sustainable Agriculture ❗

Farming practices can be criticized for their dependence on external inputs such as fuel, agricultural chemicals like pesticides and fertilizers, and the effects of farming on soil erosion and local water usage. As soils become depleted and water becomes the earth's most precious commodity, a new movement has grown and spread to conserve and protect these resources.

Conservation is the practice of preserving and carefully managing the environment and its natural resources. A new method of farming, **conservation agriculture**, has become increasingly important as a way of providing a sustainable farming system without sacrificing crop production.

Geography: Its Nature and Perspectives

Here are some examples of conservational agriculture as practiced on today's farms:

Conservation method	What it is	How it helps
No-tillage	Not plowing (or tilling) soil	Reduces soil erosion and increases fertility by retaining natural vegetation
Crop rotation	Growing a different crop on the same land in different seasons	Replenishes soil nutrients, discourages pests from sticking around, and strengthens soil by growing varying root structures
Interplanting crops	Planting fast-growing crops alongside slow-growing crops, so farmers can harvest fast-growing crops before slow-growing crops shade them out	Similar to crop rotation: Increases soil fertility and discourages pests

Sustainable yield describes the quantity of crops or animals that can be raised without endangering local resources such as soil, irrigation, or groundwater; it can also describe what can be raised without too many expensive inputs that would make farming unprofitable. Thus, **sustainability** can be viewed in both environmental and economic terms. Either way, by reducing inputs and using ecologically sound methods, farmers can reduce the risk that their farming practices may lead to long-term environmental or economic problems.

Interconnections Between and Among Places and Regions ❶

Every place on Earth is related in some way, and we have specific terminology to describe those relationships. There are a number of political geography terms such as nation and state that we use in

---

Apparently it *doesn't* take a tillage to conserve natural resources! HONK!

everyday speech as synonyms. However, the technical definitions of these terms have specific and important meaning in the geography of politics. Here's how to keep them straight:

Country

an identifiable land area

Nation

a population with a single culture (**culture group**)

State

a population under a single government (implies sovereign territory)

Nation-state

a single culture under a single government

Sovereign territory

a state is fully independent from outside control, holds territory, and that it has international recognition from other states or the United Nations

We'll take a deeper dive into these topics in Chapter 4, Political Organizations of Space.

You Need to Know the EU

The European Union (EU) is a common topic in both the multiple-choice and free-response question sections. Make sure you are familiar with all things EU—especially the latest updates about who's in and who's out. We'll get into more detail about the EU and other multinational organizations in Chapter 4, so be sure to read the text below and also head over there for more information.

Conflict and Cooperation Among Countries ❶

As an example of nations cooperating with one another, let's take a look at the European Union (EU) as the world's largest economy:

EU governance has been successful in creating a singular economy through free trade, open borders, free movement of labor, free exchange of currency, and a level playing field for business and labor in terms of laws and regulations. Instead of more than 25 small economies*, the EU acts as one state economy that is highly competitive with the United States, Japan, and emerging economies such as Russia, China, India, Brazil, or a proposed Free Trade Zone of the Americas. In terms of total gross domestic product (GDP), the International Monetary Fund reported in 2014 that the EU had an economy of nearly $18.5 trillion, while the GDP of the U.S. was approximately $17 trillion.

 * See? It's true—the farmer and the cowman CAN be friends!

Key Geographical Skills

When you think of geography, maps are probably the first things that come to mind. There is a lot to know about maps—what types of maps exist, how they represent data, how regions are defined—and lots more! In this section, we'll cover the most important map properties and geographical skills you'll be asked about on the exam.

Maps and Spatial Data

For geographers, maps are important because they are what separate us from other social scientists, such as sociologists or political scientists. Maps are not just a graphic art form; they are a science. Many scientific maps are the results of spatial data analysis—the mathematical analysis of one or more quantitative geographic patterns.

Reference Maps: Let's Get Physical, Political

The two main types of maps are **political** and **physical.** Nowadays, you'll see many maps, particularly globes and other 3-D representations, that are some creative hybrid of the two.

UNITED STATES OF AMERICA

Political maps show human-created features, such as boundaries, cities, roads, and highways. Political maps often us vibrant, distinct colors to help our eyes easily distinguish boundaries between places.

Physical maps display the geography of a place, or the natural features of the Earth. These maps often use shaded relief to show the configuration and height of land surface features, such as mountains, rivers, valleys, and deserts.

Thematic Maps ❗

A number of different map types can be grouped under the heading **thematic maps.** Remember that each one expresses a particular subject and does not show land forms for other features. The theme could be something like a **dot-density map** showing the distribution of population within a country. It could also be very complex, showing multiple related subjects, such as a weather map that shows temperature contour lines (isotherms), wind patterns, pressure zones, and areas of precipitation. The table on the following page details a few common types of thematic maps.

Thematic Map	Expression	How it works	Example
Chloropleth	Uses color variations to indicate the geographic variability of a particular theme.	Colorized symbols, contour areas filled with different colors, or polygons denoting country boundaries are filled with different colors.	Population density map with each country shaded a color representing the number of people it contains.
Dot-density	Uses dots to express the volume and density of a particular geographic feature.	Dots can represent the number of people in an area, or can express the number of events or phenomena that occurred in an area. Each dot may represent one event or multiple occurrences.	Heart Attack Density Map with dots representing the number of people who suffer heart attacks on a state-by-state basis. Each state would have a number of dots inside its boundary polygon representing the number of heart attacks.

Thematic Map	Expression	How it works	Example
Graduated Symbol	Uses the visual variable of size to represent differences in the magnitude of spatially changing phenomenon.	Similar to a dot map, but may use a different symbol that resembles what the data represent (for example, a tree symbol to represent forest density across a state or country).	A map of the U.S. with varying-sized Twitter logos representing the density c Twitter users by state.

Thematic Map	Expression	How it works	Example
Isoline	Calculates data values between points across a variable surface and expresses lines of constant value, using isoline contours.	Data is labeled with a value at each measured point. Then these points are interpolated with neighboring points to create a continuous surface of isoline contours.	Weather maps showing temperature contours (isotherms) are the most common isoline maps.

Thematic Map	Expression	How it works	Example
Cartogram	Uses a thematic variable (population, time, participation) as a substitute for distance or land area in a map.	Maps become distorted (but still recognizable) as they showcase the information.	A map of the United States features all 48 contiguous states sized to convey population data by state.

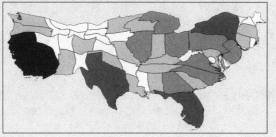

Map Projections

A map projection is a mathematical method by which one transfers the Earth's sphere onto a flat surface. That is, making a map, and as we just saw, there are many types of maps that one can make! There probably won't be a question that asks you to differentiate between the projections on the AP Human Geography Exam, but they could ask you about the practical issues behind certain projections. Each given projection creates different levels of accuracy in terms of size and shape distortion for different parts of the earth.

Remember!

Decisions, Decisions: A map projection's level of accuracy is based upon two concepts: **area preservation** and **shape preservation**.

Equal-area projections attempt to maintain the relative spatial science and the areas on the map. However, these can distort the actual shape of polygons, such as the **Lambert projection** bending and squishing the northern Canadian islands to keep them at the same map scale as southern Canada on a flat sheet of paper.

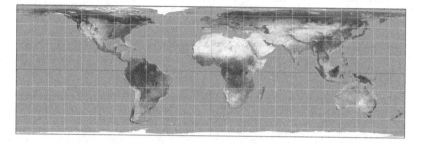

Conformal projections attempt to maintain the shape of polygons on the map. The downside is that conformal projections can cause the distortion of the relative area from one part of the map to the other. For instance, in the commonly used **Mercator projection**, the shape of Greenland is preserved, but it appears to be much larger than South America, when in reality it is much smaller.

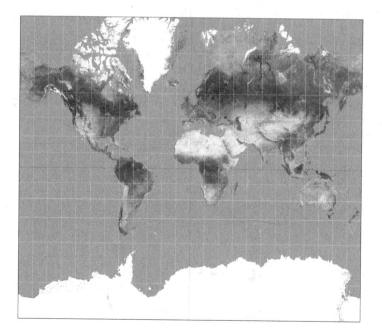

The **azimuthal equidistant projection**, or **polar projection**, maintains proportionately correct distances for all points on the map from the center point (pole). This map is useful because all lines of longitude are straight, facilitating global communication by making it easy to aim directional antennae between locations.

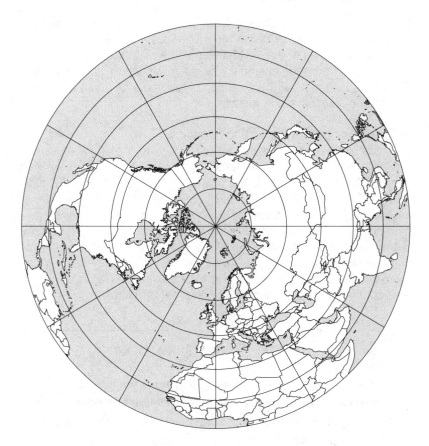

Interpreting Scales/Relationships Among Patterns ❶

Population Pyramids ❶

Population pyramids are a graphical way to visualize the **population structure** of a country or place. More specifically, population pyramids reveal the **gender** and **age distribution** of the population. Like a country's position on the Demographic Transition Model, which you'll see in Chapter 6, the shape of the pyramid can tell you a lot about that country's level of economic development.

General Principles of Population Pyramids

Look over to the right at those population pyramids. Soak it in—then read this paragraph. Ready? OK. Males are always on the left of the pyramid and females are on the right. Each bar is an age **cohort,** generally made up of five-year sets: 0–4, 5–9, 10–14, and so on. The origin (0-value) of each bar graph is the center and increases in value as you move left or right outward from the center. The single colored bar right or left of the origin is an **age-sex cohort**, with just one gender of that age group. (Note that age-sex cohorts may not always be colored on the exam.) When comparing the number of males and females in a population of cohort, the sex ratio tells you the number of males per 100 females.

Mind the Gap!

Gaps, where there is an unexpectedly small bar, are important to recognize. A gap in a male cohort but not in females of the same age group is most commonly a sign of a past war that was fought *outside the country*. A gap in data for both males and females is likely a sign of past war *inside that country*, epidemic disease, or famine.

AP Human Geography calling! The population pyramid is one pyramid scheme that you can get into without annoying your friends....

Not all population pyramids look the same. Depending upon who drew them, there may or may not be a column down the middle. Seeing the overall shape of the pyramid is what's important. We'll use both methods here so that you are used to seeing it both ways. You never know what they are going to put on the exam.

Check the Type of Data
Be aware of whether the bars on the graph show the *percent* of the total population or the total *number* of people in the age-sex cohort.

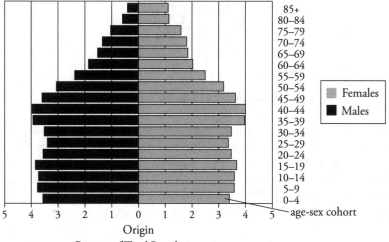

Percent Age-Sex Structure of Indiana in 2000

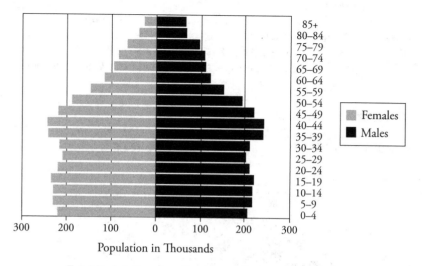

Population in Thousands

Total Population Age-Sex Structure For Indiana 2000

While those two pyramids look the same, we need to be sure when referring to the data that we recognize what kind of numbers (percent or total) we are talking about—this is especially important if asked on the essay section. What about those pyramids with the column down the middle? Those are showing the same data--they just have the number line located in a different place.

Here is what the percent data would look like:

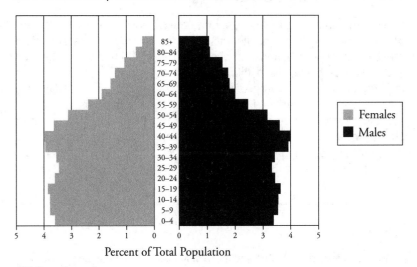

Percent of Total Population

Percent Age-Sex Structure of Indiana in 2000 With Central Column

Shape as Shorthand

The general shape of the pyramid is what tells you about the character of the country, state, province, or city that is being diagrammed. In the case of countries, pyramid shapes are indicators of growth rates and of the level of economic development. Look at the diagram below to see the generalized differences:

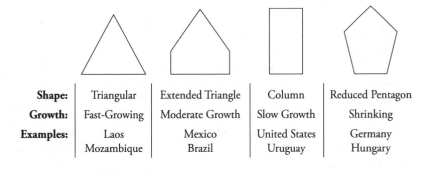

Shape:	Triangular	Extended Triangle	Column	Reduced Pentagon
Growth:	Fast-Growing	Moderate Growth	Slow Growth	Shrinking
Examples:	Laos	Mexico	United States	Germany
	Mozambique	Brazil	Uruguay	Hungary

Regions—Brass Tacks 🔵

When geographers talk about regions, they're talking about **space** and **place**. Space meaning the geometric surface of the Earth and place meaning an area of bounded space that has some importance. **Regions are a type of place and a city**, for example, can be part of multiple regions all at once. Example: Boston is considered part of New England, is also the heart of Red Sox nation, and is part of the eastern seaboard region. Another region is the **Corn Belt**—a few Midwestern states where corn has been the predominant crop since around 1850. These towns boast many family farms, many jobs in farming, and many powerful farm organizations with lobbying power.

Gimme a Hint(erland)

Note that suburban Boston and much of Massachusetts can be seen as a **hinterland** of the port in Boston. Hinterland is the area behind a port where provisions and supplies are delivered to be distributed in that area. It sounds like an old timey word, hinterland, but you should be familiar with it for the AP Human Geo Exam.

Types of Regions 🔵

There are three categories of regions that you should know for the AP Human Geography Exam:

formal
functional
vernacular

Keep in mind that there are many different types of regions, and a single place can exist in several regions simultaneously. For example, the Everglades in Florida exist within the Southern U.S. region and are also considered a wetland region. Regions exist at many different scales and can overlap. Keep an open mind about what can be considered a region.

Formal Regions

A **formal region** is an area of bounded space that possesses some **homogeneous characteristic** or **uniformity**—across the region there is at least one thing that is the same everywhere within the regional boundary.

Types of Formal Regions ❶

The defining homogeneous character can be as simple as a common language. In a **linguistic region,** everyone speaks the same language, but groups in that region can be very different culturally. Example: The United States and Australia are in the same linguistic region, but the two countries share little else in culture, economy, or landscape. Regional concepts can also be very complex. The American South or "Dixie" is one such region; a multitude of factors define the region (dialect, vocabulary, food, architecture, climate, ethnicity, religion). Because these defining characteristics are imprecise, people disagree over whether states like Virginia, West Virginia, and/or Maryland are parts of Dixie.

Regional boundaries differ based upon the type of region. **Culture regions** tend to have fuzzy borders. It's hard to tell where one region ends and the other begins, such as the border between Dixie and "the North" in the United States. Boundaries between **political regions** are finite and well-defined. Some political boundaries are porous, such as those between Canada and the United States, and other boundaries are protected, such as that between the United States and Mexico.

Environmental region boundaries are transitional and measurable. The environmental transition zone between two **bioregions,** or **biomes,** is known as an **ecotone.** Example: The ecotone between the Sahara Desert and the tropical savanna of Africa is a dry grassland region known as the Sahel.

Functional Regions

Functional regions or **nodal regions** are areas that have a **central place** or **node** that is a focus or point of origin that expresses some practical purpose. The influence of this point is strongest in the areas close to the center, and the strength of influence diminishes as distance increases from that point.

 ## *Did You Know?*

Hey There, Sports Fans!

Market areas are a type of functional region. A professional sports team will have the strongest fan base and intensive media network coverage in areas close to the team's home city. There are fans and media viewing in the larger region around that city, but they diminish as you get farther and farther away. Eventually you reach a point where the fans transition to another team's functional region and the media networks are oriented in that direction.

Vernacular Regions

The **vernacular region** is based upon the perception or collective **mental map** of the region's residents. The overall concept can vary within the region due to personal or group variations. Looking again at the American South, or "Dixie," some residents define it by the location of country music bands or fans, where others recognize the numbers of Southern Baptist church congregations or NASCAR races as the defining statistic. There are those who consider Dixieland only as the states of the Civil War—era Confederacy or the part of the country where it never (or almost never) snows. No matter what is used to spatially define the regional concept, the reason tends to be a point of pride for residents.

Be careful with your vernacular definitions. There are country music radio stations in all fifty U.S. states and throughout Canada (ever heard of Shania Twain? She's from Ontario!). Some of NASCAR's events with the largest attendance are in decidedly un-Southern states like Wisconsin, California, and New Hampshire.

Geographic Technology 🛑

Geographic Information Systems (GIS)

Geographic Information Systems (GIS) became practical with the onset of the desktop computer in the 1970s. GIS incorporate one or more **data layers** in a computer program capable of spatial analysis and mapping. Data layers are numerical, coded, or textual data that is attributed to specific geographic coordinates or areas. As all data is geographically tied to specific locations, data between layers can be analyzed spatially. Each layer can show a different type of geographic feature.

Global Positioning System (GPS)

Global Positioning System (GPS) utilizes a worldwide network of satellites, which emit a measurable radio signal. When this signal is available from three or more **Navstar** satellites, a GPS receiver is able to triangulate a coordinate location and display map data for the user. In addition, there are handheld GPS units for outdoor sporting use, GPS units on delivery trucks and emergency vehicles that notify supervisors of their location, and units that land surveyors use to locate property lines, and buried utility lines, and accurately lay out new construction sites.

Remote Sensing

Large-scale aerial photographs are commonly used by local governments to record property data and set tax assessments. Aerial photographs can also be used to revise topographic map data without having to send out a survey team to update old maps. Remote sensing is currently used to monitor the loss of wetlands and barrier islands on the Gulf Coast of Louisiana. Each year, satellite data are collected and compared with GIS to show the areas and patterns of wetland and beach loss. is analysis is used by engineers and environmental planners to develop wetland and beach restoration projects.

Chapter 1 Key Terms

rate of natural increase (RNI)
immigration
emigration
Demographic Transition Model
rank-size rule
distance decay
relative distance
Tobler's Law
friction of distance
The Isolated State Model
Latin American City Model
Theory of Industrial Location
Central Place Theory
Von Thunen's Land Use Model
Central Business District (CBD)
Industrial Location Theory
central place theory
market areas
hinterlads
Christaller's Central Place Theory
urban hierarchy
scale
map scale
relative scale
scale of analysis
level of aggregation
location
absolute location
relative location
International Date Line
space
activity space
place
toponym
area of bounded space
types of places
sequent occupancy
pattern

cluster
agglomeration
sinuous
random
scattered
linear
land survey patterns
metes and bounds
township and range
long lots
diffusion patterns
hearth
human-environment relationships
  (human ecology)
food web
food chain
conservation
sustainable yield
sustainability
country
state
nation
nation-state
sovereign territory
european Union (EU)
political maps
physical maps
thematic maps
dot-density map
chloropleth map
dot map
graduated symbol map
isoline map
cartogram map
area preservation
shape preservation
equal-area projections
Lambert projection

Chapter 1 Key Terms

conformal projections
Mercator projection
Azimuthal Equidistant Projection
 (Polar Projection)
population structure
cohort
age-sex cohort
regions: formal, functional,
 vernacular
linguistic region

regional boundaries
culture regions
political regions
environmental region
bioregions (biomes)
ecotone
functional regions (nodal regions)
vernacular region
mental map

CHAPTER 2

Population and Migration

This chapter is intended to help you better understand the dynamics, growth, and change of populations. First, we'll go over some population patterns and different ways to describe them. Then, we'll review some basic math tools to help you recall many of the complicated statistics and numerical indicators. Finally, we'll discuss how population moves, including types and implications of migration.

Geographical Analysis of Population ❗

How are populations distributed? How do we determine these patterns? And what does this mean in the larger scheme of Human Geography? We'll answer these questions, and more, in the following sections.

Population Density, Distribution, and Scale ❗

🗨 There are two main ways to calculate population density:

arithmetic density and
physiologic density.

The number of people per square unit of land is known as **arithmetic density**. Most island nations and microstates have extremely high arithmetic densities. Consider also the high arithmetic densities of countries such as India, Bangladesh, Japan, and South Korea.

 Did You Know?

Holy High Rise! If everyone on Earth lived as densely as they do in Manhattan, New York, the whole human race could fit in New Zealand!

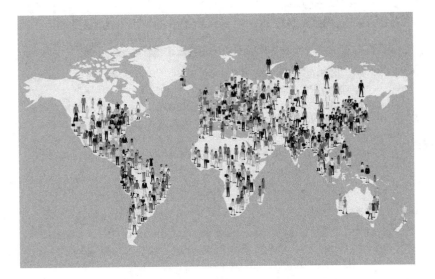

⚇ The number of people per square unit of farmland is known as the **physiologic density**. Physiologic density can be seen as a more practical tool in understanding the sustainability of a population of a certain region or country. Physiologic density is especially important in understanding the geography of countries where the amount of arable land, land usable for farming, is limited.

Limits to physiologic density can include overcrowding on farms or a lack of abundant farming regions due to geography. For example, Iraq, Egypt, Uzbekistan, and Pakistan are all arid countries that have narrow farming regions around river systems and deltas.

In countries like the United States and China, arable land sits in the eastern third of the country and the west is dominated by mountain and desert regions. There, high physiologic densities in farming regions have led to populations being squeezed into cities or westward into grassland and arid regions to expand agriculture to new areas.

Factors Explaining Patterns of Population Distribution—Physical and Human 🔴

Population distribution is affected by many factors—birth rate, death rate, emigration, immigration, war, famine, outbreaks, and more. Newly Industrialized Countries (NICs) often experience rapid internal rural-to-urban migration. This migration is inspired by two types of factors:

- **push factors** are specific things about rural life that force people off farms and into cities
- **pull factors** are specific things about cities that draw people to them.

Some **physical factors** influence population distribution: climate (think about all of those grandparents retiring down to Florida for good weather year round), land forms and bodies of water (affecting whether it's feasible to move to a certain location or impossible). In addition, **human factors** affect population distribution: culture (perhaps you get a new job in a region that you don't know too well and you worry, *will I feel welcome and accepted there?*), economics *(are there jobs that pay enough in that area? Is there housing that's reasonably priced?),* historical (are you an Existentialism buff? Then Concord, Massachusetts, may be calling your name), political (if you wish to be surrounded by people of the same mindset, you might pick a famously conservative or liberal city).

Implications of Various Densities and Distributions 🔴

Environmental and Natural Resources 🔴

The most important concept to understand about the sustainability of the global population is **carrying capacity**. On a global scale, how many people can the Earth sustain? What is the capacity on a regional scale?

Across the ecumene*, the living space of humans on the Earth's surface, there are certain limits to how many people an environment can support in terms of the availability of food, water, and natural resources. Some regions support human settlement better than others. For instance, temperate grasslands support far more people than deserts do. That seems obvious, but why then are so many people, in this day and age, moving in greater number into arid regions (such as the south western region of the United States)? Second, how long before dry regions are pushed to their limits, especially in terms of fresh water?

Overpopulation is a major concern both in resource-poor regions and across the globe. Certain resources such as clean water, endangered plant and animal habitats, and nonrenewable energy sources (such as oil) will be depleted if conservation efforts and population control methods are not mandated by governments. Some theorists have expressed a need for the goal of zero population growth worldwide to stem the tide of resource depletion. To do this, some have proposed large-scale family planning and contraceptive programs. However, many have rejected these ideas based primarily on religious or political beliefs.

Another benefit arising from population control would be alleviating concerns over decreasing amounts of personal space as population densities increase. Some worry that too many people crammed into densely packed urban areas will lead to social unrest and, potentially, armed conflicts.

Other population theorists have examined the role of conservation in global population sustainability. To achieve sustainable resource use in coming decades, with an expected 10 billion person global population, massive and systematic global programs enforcing recycling, energy conservation, sustainable farming practices, and a wholesale reduction of personal consumption are believed to be necessary. Without conservation, many resources could be depleted before we have the chance to save them.

---

 *What the ecumene?? Ecumene is just a term used by geographers to mean "inhabited land" but doesn't it sound wicked smart?

Searching for information on Population Composition and Population Pyramids? These topics are connected to this material, so flip back to Chapter 1 for more in-depth coverage.

Population Growth and Decline Over Time and Space 🗲

Population growth is understood through an examination of historical trends and projection of those trends into the future. Several models exist to predict population growth, such as the **Demographic Transition Model, Malthusian theory,** and the **Epidemiologic Transition Model.** The demographic equation uses birth rates and death rates along with immigration and emigration statistics to show population growth or change. Over the next few pages, we will walk you through the process of how population growth is calculated.

Historical Trends and Future Projections 🗲

We've talked a lot about the concepts of population change, but you'll also need to know a few basic equations that allow us to crunch the numbers. Read on to find out exactly how we quantify population growth and decline.

Demographic Equation

The **demographic equation** is the most commonly used method to calculate population growth. Using annual birth rates and death rates to calculate the natural increase in overall population (note that we're not talking about the "rate" of natural increase here, just the total number of people), we can add the balance to the **net migration rate (NMR)**. This is the number of immigrants minus the number of emigrants for every thousand members of the population. Here is the formula used to calculate the net migration rate:

$$\text{NMR} = \frac{\text{Number of Immigrants} - \text{Number of Emigrants}}{\text{Population} \div 1,000}$$

Take this and add it to the birth rate minus the death rate and you will have total population growth per thousand members of the population. Thus, you have your demographic equation, like so:

$$\frac{(\text{Birth Rate} - \text{Death Rate}) + \text{Net Migration Rate}}{10} = \frac{\text{Population Growth}}{\text{Percentage Rate}}$$

Did You Know?

Shrinkage: The United States has a birth rate of 13 and a death rate of 8. Add the product to a net migration rate of 2.45 and we find that the United States adds about 7.5 people for every thousand in the population, annually. Divide by 10 to find that the population growth rate (including immigra-tion) is 0.75 percent annually.

 Do you have a tough time remembering the difference between immigrants and emigrants? Remember it this way: *Immigrants* come *in* to a country. *Emmigrants exit* a country.

Fertility Rate ❶

By definition, the **total fertility rate (TFR)** is the estimated average number of children born to each female of birthing age (15 to 45).

We can still use a basic formulaic definition to help remember TFR:

$$\text{TFR} = \frac{\text{Number of Children Born}}{\text{Women Aged 15 to 45}}$$

However, the TFR is not an annual statistic (like the RNI, or Rate of Natural Increase introduced in Chapter 1). It is more of an estimate, taken as a snapshot of fertility for birth over the prior 30 years. Thus, TFR and RNI are not comparable. There cannot be a negative TFR, for one thing. TFR highlights the importance of replacement in the population.

But Wait, There's More...

More demographic factors influencing population growth, that is. For information on Rates of Natural Increase and Population-Doubling Time, both of which are important for your exam, please put it in reverse and head back to Chapter 1 (but be careful to check your rearview mirror!).

Theories of Population Growth ❶

There are three main theories of Population Growth and we name dropped them a few pages back, but now we're going to dig in. Those three main theories are:

- The Demographic Transition Model
- Malthusian Theory
- The Epidemiologic Transition Model

Let's explore all three, shall we?

Demographic Transition Model ❶

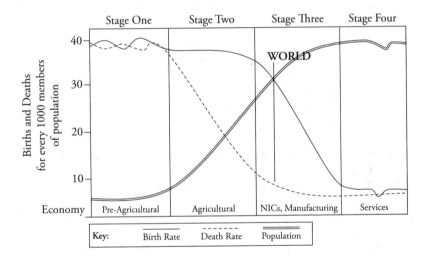

The **Demographic Transition Model** has a number of uses. You should think of it as a central unifying concept in your understanding of the AP Human Geography course. Not only is it a theory of how population changes over time, but it also provides important insights into issues of migration, fertility, economic development, industrialization, urbanization, labor, politics, and the roles of women.

By placing a country on the model, you are defining the **population dynamics** and **economic context** of that country. Knowing where a country falls on the model lets you know what kind of economy the country has, whether or not there is significant migration going on, and, like economic indicators, this "picture" of a country's population can tell you much about its quality of life. These are theoretical estimates and averages, and not all countries fit the model perfectly.

The model also has a **predictive capability** (just like that crystal ball seen above). If a country currently falls within Stage Two of the transition, we can use this model to predict how its population will change over time and speculate as to how much it can grow in size. Likewise, you can also look at the whole world, which falls into early Stage Three. Knowing this, we can estimate a **population projection** that the planet's population has reached only about two-thirds of its potential. If the planet is currently at about 7.2 billion people, then we can expect that once global populations level off in Stage Four, global population will be somewhere around 10 billion people. This may happen in your lifetime, sometime around 2060.

The DTM (that's what the cool kids call the Demographic Transition Model) also provides insight into economic history (see the graph on the next page). If we look at the United States, Canada, or Western Europe, we can apply dates to the bottom of the model to show how Stage Four countries have progressed through the system. Looking at the model on the next page, we can see in Western Europe the beginning of the Renaissance; in Western Europe and in the United States and Canada, the **Industrial Revolution**; and likewise the recent **deindustrialization** or shift to **service-based economies**.

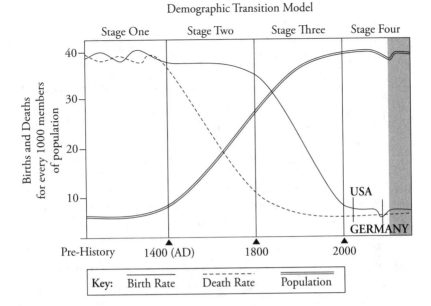

Demographic Transition Model

Pre-history goes all the way back to human beginnings. Fourteen hundred represents the time when there was both a cultural and economic renaissance in Europe. Eighteen hundred represents the Industrial Revolution, when countries like the United States and Great Britain were **newly industrialized countries (NICs).** And 2000 represents a turning point of the rise of service-based economies of **more developed countries (MDCs).** The typical MDC has a birth rate of 11 and a death rate of 10, or very little growth.

Countries that are not as demographically or economically advanced can also be placed on the model, but you have to change the dates as to when they reach the significant turning point in their history. If we look at newly industrialized countries (NICs) such as Brazil, Mexico, and India, we can see a much more recent turning point from the **agricultural economy** of Stage Two to the **manufacturing-based economy** of Stage Three.

One Size Doesn't Fit All

Remember, this is a theoretical model and not all countries fit the trend. For example, China, due to its one-child policy, appears far more advanced than it should be, compared economically to other NICs.

You've probably noticed that the population line in the model has a distinct shape to it until stage four. This is what demographers (population scientists) and population biologists call the **S-curve**. Humans are not the only ones whose population follows such a pattern. In fact, give any animal population a vast amount of food or remove predators from their habitat and you will see rapid population growth followed by a plateau or decline due to a population reaching or exceeding the area's **carrying capacity.** Globally, humans may be doing the same thing and the human population may reach **equilibrium** in the global habitat.

Below is a summary of each stage of the Demographic Transition Model and its characteristics. You'll definitely want to know these for the exam.

	Birth Rates	Death Rates	Life Expectancy	RNI
Stage One	High (25–50)	High (25–40)	Low (33–50)	Low–Moderate (–0.1–1.9%)
Stage Two	High (25–50)	Decreasing (8–25)	Increasing (<70)	Highest (1.5–3.5%)
NICs	Decreasing (12–30)	Lowering (5–18)	Increasing (<75)	Higher (1.1–2.7%)
Stage Three	Lowering (12–20)	Low (5–12)	Higher (<78)	Lowering (0.5–1.2%)
Stage Four	Low (8–16)	Low (5–12)	Highest (<82)	Low to Negative (0.8 to –0.6%)

Malthusian Theory

Englishman Thomas Malthus published *An Essay on the Principle of Population* in 1798. His main idea was that the global population would one day expand to the point where it could not produce enough food to feed everyone. He predicted this would happen before 1900. The Malthusian catastrophe did not happen by 1900 or even by today, but some more recent thinkers (neo-Malthusians) think it still could in the future.

Why did he have this idea? At the time the math made sense, as the United Kingdom was engaged in the Industrial Revolution and people were being born at a high rate. If we look at the Demographic Transition Model timeline, Britain was moving from stage two to stage three. Like we see in NICs of today, Malthus saw rapid migration to the cities and a population explosion.

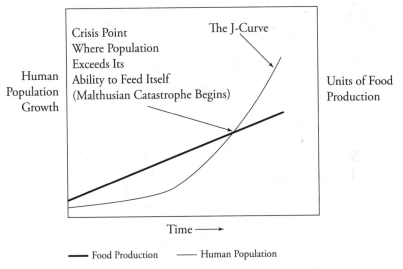

Malthus's Prediction Regarding Population and Food Production

Mathematically, what Malthus saw was that food production did grow over time, but in a slow arithmetic manner. Arithmetic growth means that each year another unit of food production was added to the overall volume of agricultural products*. Meanwhile, human population grows in an exponential manner. Exponential growth means that a couple has a few children and then their children all have a few children, and so on through generations. Every few decades, you have population + the population, resulting in a logistic curve, or **J-curve,** of exponential population growth on the graph. Looking at the numbers of the time, Malthus believed that the population was going to catch up with agricultural production quickly.

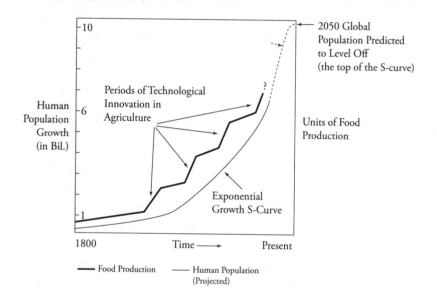

Human Population Growth (in Bil.)

10

6

1

Periods of Technological Innovation in Agriculture

?

2050 Global Population Predicted to Level Off (the top of the S-curve)

Units of Food Production

Exponential Growth S-Curve

1800   Time ⟶   Present

—— Food Production   —— Human Population (Projected)

*Think of this like a volume + 1 situation or a constant rate of change from algebra class. Wait, there's math on this test? Don't worry, not much!

It wasn't that Malthus was wrong, but that he couldn't have predicted that agricultural technology was going to boost food production several times over in the coming century. By 1900, massively important inventions such as the internal combustion engine, artificial fertilizers, pesticides, irrigation pumps, advanced plant and animal hybridization techniques, the tin can, and refrigeration were developed. As each of these new products and methods were adopted, another large volume of food would be added to global production and supply. Mathematically, this meant that food production has continued to stay ahead of population growth. For how long this will occur, we don't know. Let's hope that by 2050 or so, when the global population is predicted to level off around 10 billion (completing the top of the S-curve), that the world has food production in good working order.

 Ask Yourself...

What About Genetics? Avoid the Trap!

In the early 1800s, Gregor Mendel was the first to research and write about genes and plant reproduction. However, the science of genetics did not make any impact on global food production until the 1950s and genetically modified foods did not enter markets until the 1980s. If you are asked about why Malthus was wrong, perhaps in an essay question, talk about new technologies including plant and animal hybrids, but not genetics, since that affects agriculture only in much more recent years.

Epidemiologic Transition Model ❶

Closely linked to the Demographic Transition Model is the Epidemiological Transition Model, which specifically accounts for development due to the increasing population growth rates caused by medical advances. In the ETM, the phase of development is directly followed by a stabilization of population growth as the procreation rates decline.

Causes and Implication of an Aging Population ❶

As modern people's life expectancy grows, the characteristics of the world's population evolve as well. We'll discuss the causes and consequences of our aging population in this section.

Birth Rates ❶

Natality, which is the **crude birth rate (CBR)** (aka the birth rate) is an **annual statistic.** The total number of infants born living is counted for one calendar year and then calculated. This figure is then divided by the population divided by one thousand, or "every thousand members of the population," as it is often presented. Why? By standardizing the denominator (you probably know about common denominators from math class), the resulting quotient will be a small integer number, such as 32 or 14. This makes the data much easier to work with.

$$\text{CBR} = \frac{\text{Number of Live Births}}{\text{Total Population}} \times 1,000$$

Knock it Off!

So if you have a country with 100,000 live births in a year and a population of 5,000,000, the birth rate is 20; more precisely 20 live births for every 1,000 members of the population. To make this easier, 5,000,000 divided by 1,000 is 5,000.

Knock the 3 zeros off the end of 1,000 and the end of 5,000,000 and you have a simplified ratio of 5,000/1 or just 5,000. Do the same with 100,000 over 5,000. Knock off the three zeros of each and you have 100/5 or 20.

Birth rate is just one piece of the larger demographic picture. High birth rates (18 to 50) are found in mostly rural agricultural Third-World countries and low birth rates (8 to 17) are more likely to be found in urbanized industrial and service-based economies. However, without knowing what's going on with mortality in that country (death rate), it's hard to know whether the population is growing and, if it is, how quickly.

Death Rates ❶

Okay, it sounds scary. Death is an emotional issue. What you need to do here is to think scientifically about these statistics. The mortality rate, also known as the crude death rate (CDR) or what we'll simply call the **death rate,** is an annual statistic calculated in the same way as the birth rate. The number of deaths are counted for the calendar year in a country and divided by every thousand members of the population.

$$CDR = \frac{\text{Number of Deaths}}{\text{Total Population}} \times 1,000$$

So what does the death rate tell us? Well, not much in today's world. High death rates usually indicate a country that is experiencing war, disease, or famine. Historically, higher death rates (20 to 50) were recorded in the poorest of Third-World countries where the combination of poverty, poor nutrition, epidemic disease, and a lack of medical care resulted in low **life expectancy.** However, as conditions have improved in the Third World through the **Green Revolution** (increased food and nutrition) and access to sanitation, education, and health care have increased, life expectancies have gone up, and the death rate has gone down.

Social, Economic, and Political Implications ❶

An aging population can have social, economic, and political implications. In the United States presently, we are experiencing a demographic shift in which over the next few decades, the number of Americans who are older than 65 is expected to more than double. This shift is the result of rising longevity and is part of a larger shift in the age profile of the United States, partially caused by families having fewer children.

The economic implications of this shift are quite worrisome. Thanks to these longer life expectancies and lower birth rates, social programs such as Social Security, Medicare, Medicaid are burdened with many beneficiaries but fewer contributors paying into these programs via taxes. Some fear that the government will even increase taxes (a political implication of this growing, "greying" population) in order to cover the growing costs of this group.

In addition, a population that finds itself living longer will likely seek to work longer, so the average retirement age may creep up and there may be more stagnation at the top of companies, with corporate leaders sticking around longer than they did in generations past. This can affect the career trajectory of the next generation and have resultant economic implications.

Types of Migration ❗

Voluntary

Migration can take many forms—**interregional** or **internal migrants** move from one region of a country to another where as **transnational migrants** move from one country to another. Voluntary migrants may be seeking better jobs or opportunities or programs (public schools or transportation options). **Step migration** occurs when people move up in a hierarchy of locations—perhaps from farm to small town, then from small town to regional city, then from regional city to major city. **Chain migration** occurs when a pioneering migrant or group settles in a new place and then encourages his or her friends or family to move to this location, also. This chain migration can end up turning certain areas into successful immigrant communities.

Involuntary

But not all migration is as deliberate and inspiring as the examples above. Some migration is involuntary or what is called **forced migration.** Governments can order their citizens to move from one place to another (an example of this is if a government wishes to build a large highway through a formerly residential area). Other people who are are forced to move by war, disasters, or fear of government repression are called **refugees.** Other, more stable countries may grant those refugees **asylum** and offer them the opportunity to apply for official status or citizenship.

 Ask Yourself...

Think of some examples (either from present day news or from your history textbook) of voluntary migration and involuntary migration and marinate on them, as you might need to be familiar with those for an essay prompt.

Chapter 2 Key Terms

arithmetic density
physiologic density
push factors
pull factors
physical factors
human factors
carrying capacity
overpopulation
Demographic Transition Model
Malthusian Theory
Epidemiologic Transition Model
demographic equation
net migration rate (NMR)
total fertility rate (TFR)
population dynamics
economic context
predictive capability

population projection
Industrial Revolution
deindustrialization
service-based economies
Newly Industrialized Countries (NICs)
More Developed Countries (MDCs)
agricultural economy
manufacturing-based economy
S-curve
carrying capacity
equilibrium
J-curve
Crude Birth Rate (CBR)
annual statistic
death rate
life expectancy
Green Revolution

CHAPTER 3

Cultural Patterns and Processes

This chapter is intended to help you better understand the diversity of cultures across the globe. **Culture** is the shared experience, traits, and activities of a group of people who have a common heritage. While a definition of culture technically exists, it's an abstract concept, so in this chapter we'll give you the many components of the cultural landscape.

Whether something is original to a single culture or is the product of cultural synthesis, it is important to understand the underpinnings of the things we see in the cultural landscape. Combined, the many components come together to identify and define a single **culture group** or **nation.**

What Is Culture? ❗

Art

Architecture

Language

Music

Film and Television

Food

Clothing

Social Interaction

Religion

Folklore

Land Use

The Cultural Landscape 🔱

Almost everything we see and hear in the human landscape expresses some form of culture. Culture is complex, and trying to take it all in and make sense of it can be confusing. To get a better grip on culture, we first have to understand how it is found on the **cultural landscape,** or the cultural properties that represent the combined works of nature and of man.

We can see the cultural landscape in the form of **signs** and **symbols** (representations that carry a particular meaning among those who share a culture) in the world around us—there are different ways customs are imprinted on the **components of culture.**

What we find is that some things are original to a single culture, but most things in the cultural landscape are the product of **cultural synthesis** or **syncretism**—the blending together of two or more cultural influences.

Architecture as Culture 🔱

If you can believe it, the buildings that you walk by and see every day are considered part of your "culture." Housing types and religious buildings are especially relevant.

Within the **built environment** of the human landscape, we find a multitude of **architectural forms** that are the product of cultural influence. When new buildings are constructed, much news is made over innovative designs in **modern** and **contemporary architecture.** This is in contrast to the existing forms of **traditional architecture,** some of which has been used for centuries.

Modern Architecture

Architects have a distinct modern period of architecture that differs from new, or shall we say contemporary, forms. Be specific when describing a home or building type. **Modern** means architecture developed during the twentieth century that expresses geometric, ordered forms made of steel, concrete, and glass with few frivolous designs or ornate details. Architectural forms such as the 1950s homes of Frank Lloyd Wright (right) or the rectangular steel and glass skyscrapers built in the 1970s and 1980s. Modern architectural forms are considered the hallmark of American life.

Contemporary Architecture

Contemporary architecture of the present is organic, with the use of curvature. **Postmodern,** a category within contemporary, means that the design abandons use of blocky rectilinear shapes in favor of wavy, crystalline, or bending shapes in the architectural form. Contemporary architecture can also incorporate green energy technologies, recycled materials, or nontraditional materials like metal sheeting on the exterior. This is exemplified in the Frank Gehry design of the Guggenheim Museum in Bilbao, Spain, or the Walt Disney Theater in Los Angeles (left).

Traditional Architecture

Traditional architecture can express one of two types of buildings: commercial or housing. One form of traditional architecture seen in new **commercial buildings** incorporates the efficiency and simplicity of modern architecture into a standard building design with squared walls and utilizes traditional materials like stone, brick, steel, and glass. The other expression of traditional architecture is seen in housing based upon **folk house** designs from different regions of the U.S. New homes built today often incorporate more than one element of folk house design. Let's go over the basic **traditional housing style** forms that could appear on the exam.

New England: Small one-story pitched roof **Cape Cod** style or the irregular roof **Saltbox** with one long pitched roof in front and a sort of low-angle roof in back.

Federalist or Georgian: Refers to the housing styles of the late 1700s and early 1800s in Anglo-America, which are often two- or three-story urban townhomes connected to one another. Architectural elements feature classical Greek and Roman designs and stone carvings. These are symmetrical homes with central doorways and equal numbers of windows on each side of the house.

The I-house: Simple rectangular I-houses have a central door with one window on each side of the home's front and three symmetrical windows on the second floor. However, as the I-house style diffused westward, the rectangle shape and symmetry was lost. Later I-houses have the door moved to the side and have additions onto the back or side of the house. The I-house giveaways are the fireplaces on each end of the house and an even-pitched roof. The loss of form as the I-house moved across the Appalachian Mountains to the Midwest and across the Great Lakes to the Prairie Provinces is an example of **relocation diffusion.**

Religious Buildings & Places ❗

Another area of architecture the AP Human Geography Exam tests is religious architecture. Here are the major world religious groups and their representative architectural forms for places of worship.

Christian

Traditional houses of worship tend to have a central steeple or two high bell towers in the front of the building. The steeple is typical of smaller churches, and bell towers are found in larger churches and cathedrals. Basilicas, like St. Peters in the Vatican or St. Paul's Cathedral in London, have central domes similar to the U.S. Capitol building. Older churches, cathedrals, and basilicas feature a cross-shaped floor plan.

Chapel, Cathedral, Eastern Orthodox

National Cathedral, Washington, D.C.

Holy Virgin Orthodox Cathedral, San Francisco, California

Hindu

Temples and shrines tend to have a rectangular-shaped main body and feature one or more short towers of carved stone. The towers often feature stepped sides and display carvings of the heads and faces of deities. The most famous example of this design is the temple complex of Angkor Wat in Cambodia. The Kashi Vishwanath Temple in Varanasi, India, is shown to the right.

Hindu temple at Varanasi, India

Buddhist

Temples and shrines vary depending on which Buddhist tradition is followed in the region. In Nepal and Tibet, a temple can be a **stupa,** with a dome or tower featuring a pair of eyes. In East Asia, the tower-style **pagoda** with several levels that each feature winged roofs extending outward is common. Temples and shrines in China and in Shinto Japan (a Buddhist offshoot) feature one- or two-story buildings with large, curved, winged roofs (seen below). Temples are often guarded by large lion statues, such as those at the Temple of the Sun and Moon in the Forbidden City of Beijing. Temples in Southeast Asia tend to have several towers with thin pointed spires that point outward at an angle (shown to the right).

Stupa, a Type of Vajrayana (Tibet, Nepal, Bhutan)

Mahayana Buddhist Temple (China, Japan)

Theravada Buddhist Temple (Thailand)

Islamic

Mosques can take a variety of forms, though many have central domes. The giveaway feature of a mosque is one or more **minarets,** narrow towers that are pointed on top. Famous mosques include the Al-Kaaba Mosque in Mecca, the most holy place in Islam, an open-air mosque with a large black cube at its center. The third most holy place in Islam is the Al-Aqsa mosque in Jerusalem that sits alongside the Dome of the Rock, an eight-sided mosque with a high central dome and thin spire on top featuring a crescent moon. Almost all mosques are built on an angle that places the main prayer area toward Mecca.

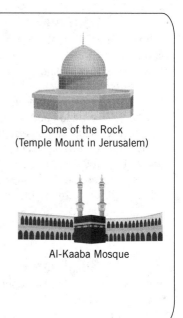

Dome of the Rock
(Temple Mount in Jerusalem)

Al-Kaaba Mosque

Judaic

There is not a common architectural design style to synagogues. The most holy place in Judaism is the Western Wall of the former Temple of Solomon, next to the Dome of the Rock. Known as the **Wailing Wall,** the old foundation walls feature large rectangular stone blocks where Jews pray and place written prayers in the cracks between the blocks.

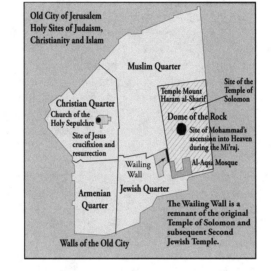

Old City of Jerusalem
Holy Sites of Judaism,
Christianity and Islam

Muslim Quarter

Site of the
Temple of
Solomon

Temple Mount
Haram al-Sharif

Christian Quarter

Church of the
Holy Sepulchre

Dome of the Rock

Site of Jesus
crucifixion and
resurrection

Site of Mohammad's
ascension into Heaven
during the Mi'raj.

Wailing
Wall

Al-Aqsa Mosque

Armenian
Quarter

Jewish Quarter

The Wailing Wall is a
remnant of the original
Temple of Solomon and
subsequent Second
Jewish Temple.

Walls of the Old City

Language As Culture ❗

Language is an important component of of culture.

In terms of **official languages,** the United States federal government has not designated one, but much of the United States tends to be **monolingual** (knowing one language—English—only). Other states such as California accept that they have a large **multilingual** immigrant population and have made provisions (especially for public safety) to provide some services in multiple languages. In Canada, there are two official languages: English and French. Therefore, Canada is **bilingual.** Depending upon where you are in a larger **linguistic region,** the way a common language is spoken can sound different, depending upon who is speaking it. In the global English linguistic region, dialect changes from nation to nation. Within a country, dialect can change from region to region (take, for example, the pronunciation of "coffee" in different areas of America).

Around the world, there are a small number of major **language families** represented by the early or prehistoric language roots. The largest members of these language families are as follows:

- Indo-European (2.9 billion people)
- Sino-Tibetan (1.3 billion people)
- Niger-Congo (435 million people)
- Afro-Asiatic (375 million people)
- Austronesian (346 million people)
- Dravidian (230 million people)
- Altaic (165 million people)
- Japanese (123 million people)
- Tai-Kadai (81 million people)

Each language family can be broken into **language groups** then into **language subfamilies** and then into smaller language groups. For example, the English language draws from the Indo-European family, Germanic subfamily, and Western Germanic group, along with German Dutch and Afrikaans. Hindi is also from the Indo-European family, but from the Indo-Iranian subfamily and Indian group along with Bengali and Nepali.

Anatolian or Kurgan—Who Ya Got?

Language change is all about migration, going all the way back to **prehistoric migrations** from the Indian subcontinent into Europe. These early immigrants brought their Indo-European root language with them, which then divided locally and evolved into the contemporary European languages of today. The Anatolian and Kurgan theories are two competing theories regarding the launching point (also called the **hearth**) of European language. It is difficult to prove whether either theory holds true, but here are the two biggest ones:

Anatolian	Kurgan
The **Anatolian theory** holds that migrants from the Indian subcontinent and their language were for some time concentrated in the peninsula that makes up most of present-day Turkey, known historically as Asia Minor or Anatolia. From there, a large migration crossed the **Hellespont** into continental Europe and spread outward into what was possibly a relatively unpopulated region. The Anatolian theory also holds that the European language was spread through agricultural innovations.	The **Kurgan theory** holds that the same group of migrants from the Indian sub-continent instead made their way into Central Asia, and then migrated across the **Eurasian steppe** into central and Western Europe, taking their language with them. In contrast to the Anatolian theory, the Kurgan theory proposes that the European language diffused through conquest.

OR

Linguistic Regions

Today **English** is accepted as the global **lingua franca,** or language used to bridge the linguistic gap between people of different national heritage, as the English language dominates popular culture media, the Internet, and the business world. However, depending upon where you are in a larger linguistic region, the way a common language is spoken can sound different, depending upon who is speaking it.

English Dialects

In the global English linguistic region, **dialect** changes from nation to nation. Although the English spoken by English people and Australian people sounds similar, there is a distinct "strain" of English spoken in Australia with a variety of different **word sounds** and **vocabulary.**

Even within Great Britain, varieties of dialect are shaped in part by national heritage. English spoken in England proper is quite different from English in the other nations or culture areas of Scotland, Wales, Ireland, Cornwall, or the Isle of Man. These variations are due in part to the degree of Celtic influence and the degree to which Anglo-Saxon invaders, who brought their Germanic language with them, settled in the region during the first millennium c.e. What some refer to as the King's English or "posh*" English is linguistically known as **received pronunciation.**

---

*The idea of something being "posh" existed before Victoria Beckham, aka Posh Spice.

Conversely, **Cockney** English is the language of the working-class areas of the East London docklands and surrounding neighborhoods, which sounds distinctly not posh. Cockney is also thought to be very influential in the formation of Australian English.

 Ask Yourself...

Think about language differences in your local area. Do you notice certain regionalisms (local accents or ways of pronouncing certain words) that differ from how you might hear a newscaster speak? Do you notice linguistic differences between blue collar and white collar citizens or different areas of your region or city?

Pidgin, Creole, and Patois 🔄

Slang, or language that is generally comprised of casual figures of speech, is similar to other heavily modified dialects of pidgin English. **Pidgin** languages are simplified forms of the language that use key vocabulary words and limited grammar. This is often heard in the spoken English of Hindustani Indian immigrants to Britain, Canada, and the United States.

Pidgin language forms can evolve into their own individual language groups over time. In Haiti, **French Creole** is spoken, which incorporates continental French with African dialectal sounds and vocabulary. In fact, many of the French overseas territories have their own forms of **patois,** like the one spoken in the islands of Martinique or Reunion, formed by local or immigrant linguistic syntheses. Pidgin, Creole, and patois can all be thought of as **syncretic language** forms that integrate both colonial and indigenous language forms.

How Does Language Evolve? ❗

We often examine how language, culture, ideas, or technology spread from a point of origin to other parts of the world and how, in that act of spreading, they evolve. There are a number of different ways and patterns in which such human phenomena diffuse spatially or spread across the Earth's surface. Back in Chapter 1, we discussed diffusion patterns on page 24. Keep in mind that language is one of those cultural signifiers that can diffuse and is subject to the myriad types of diffusion that are possible. Flip back to Chapter 1 and revisit that list before moving on.

Cultural Change ❗

The term **indigenous** means the people who were the original occupants of a place or region. The **indigenous culture** is, therefore, the original culture of that same region. The loss of indigenous culture has become a significant concern among citizens and a major policy issue among governments. In some cases, the indigenous culture is merely threatened by external cultural influences. Yet in many other cases around the world, cultures are in danger of extinction if something is not done to help protect and promote the **preservation of cultural heritage.**

Long-term cultural changes can be seen in all of the world's populated regions. One way this is observed is through the concept of **sequent occupance.** That is, for a single place or region, different dominant cultures replace each other over time. When we examine the cultural landscape of a place, we often see remnants of previous cultural influences. **Cultural adaptation** occurs when the cultural landscape retains the imprint of minority and immigrant groups. The ethnic neighborhood is the best example of how these groups make their way into the layers of sequent occupance at a much smaller scale.

 Ask Yourself...

Can you think of any examples of cultural adaptation (or a concept you may have read about--cultural appropriation) occurring currently? Are you familiar with the cultural history of your hometown or city or region?

Two Types of Cultural Adaptation

Acculturation

When the European immigrants came to America in the early part of the twentieth century they adopted many new beliefs and behaviors in their new home. They still kept much of their original culture, but they learned the American norms as they adjusted to life in America. This is an example of **acculturation**—the process of adapting to a new culture while still keeping some of one's original culture. Usually acculturation is a two-way street, with both the original and the incoming culture group swapping cultural traits.

Assimilation

Assimilation is more of an "all-or-nothing" process. Assimilation is a complete change in the identity of a minority culture group as it becomes part of the majority culture group. An example of assimilation occurred when the U.S. government adopted a policy of "forced assimilation" of the Native American population. The government forced the Native Americans to move to reservations where they were taught in government-run schools. The people were made to learn English and give up their native tongue. The government insisted they adopt the dress, manners, language, and ways of the dominant American culture. The "old ways" were forbidden. This total absorption into the dominant culture is one-way and usually "encouraged" by government policy when the new residents are forced to learn the new languages and embrace the new ways.

Look! It's a melting pot!

If this tragic era in the history of the United States interests you and you wish to learn more about the forced assimilation of Native Americans, check out *Education for Extinction: American Indians and the Boarding School Experience, 1875-1928* by David Wallace Adams or *From Deep Woods to Civilization* by Charles Alexander (Ohiyesa) Eastman.

Religion ❗

Religions, also referred to as **belief systems** by some, are as numerous as languages. Like languages, specific religions are drawn from a number of larger global groups. Categorically, religions can be characterized by their expanse: **Universalizing religions** accept followers from all ethnicities worldwide; as opposed to **ethnic religions,** which are confined to members of a specific culture group. All organized religions have one or more books of **scripture,** said to be of **divine origin,** and formal **doctrine** that governs religious practice, worship, and ethical behavior in society.

Religions and their component **denominations** can also be understood by their ability to compromise and change ideologically. **Compromising religions** are often cited for the ability to reform or integrate other beliefs into their doctrinal practices. **Fundamentalists,** on the other hand, are known to have little interest in compromising their beliefs or doctrine and strictly adhere to scriptural dictates. Know that fundamentalists tend to focus on particular relevant parts of scripture but can ignore the dictates in scriptures that may not be relevant or legal in contemporary life.

Animist Tradition

- Various ethnic, tribal, and forms of nature worship

- Though geographically unrelated, these groups have common themes, worship practices, and morality tales, which define an ethical way to live.

- **Animus** means spirit in Latin. Animists share the common belief that items in nature can have spiritual being, including landforms, animals, and trees.

Hindu-Buddhist Tradition

- The oldest universalizing religions began with Hinduism 5,000 years ago. These **polytheistic** (believing in more than one supreme god) denominations spread throughout Asia by the 1200s C.E.

- Commonalities include many levels of existence, the highest being nirvana, in which someone achieves total consciousness or enlightenment.

- One's soul is reincarnated over and over into different forms. **Karma,** the balance between good and evil deeds in life, determines the outcome of reincarnation into a lower, similar, or higher form of existence in the next life.

Abrahamic Tradition

- Judaism, Christianity, and Islam have similar scriptural descriptions of the Earth's genesis and the story of Abraham as a morality tale of respect for the will of God or Allah.

- Each religion is a **monotheistic** belief system with a singular supreme being and sub-deities such as saints, angels, archangels.

- Significance is placed upon prophecy that predicts the coming or return of a messianic figure that defeats the forces of a satanic evil for souls of followers.

Animist Religions ❶

While there are hundreds of animist belief systems, two animist religions that are commonly tested on the AP exam are Native American and Voodoun.

Native American

- Who: Pre-Columbian civilizations in the Americas and some descendants

- When: From the last period of glaciation (18,000 B.C.E.)

- Where: Alaska to the Tierra del Fuego

- Scripture: None. System based upon belief in a supreme or Great Spirit that oversees all. Shamans lead worship and provide spiritual interpretation.

- Doctrine: Depends upon tribal following. Prayers or appeals to sun, moon, animal spirits, and climatic features are significant in most practices.

- Denominations: Hundreds of different tribal interpretations

- Historical Diffusion: **Migration diffusion** north to south through the Americas

Voodoun (Voodoo)

- Who: West African; Afro-Brazilian, and Afro-Caribbean descendants
- When: Prehistory to present
- Where: Nigeria, Benin, Ghana, and other states in the region; Haiti, Cuba, Dominican Republic, Brazil, and other communities in the region.
- Scripture: None. System based upon multiple deities that control different parts of the inhabited world; shamanism is part of the system of worship.
- Doctrine: Depends upon community. Worshippers attempt to contact deities and ancestors through ceremonies, dance, and sacrificial practices.
- Denominations: Distinct differences based on region and degree of influence from Christian worship by Voodoun followers.
- Historical Diffusion: From West Africa relocation diffusion by forced migration under European-directed slavery to the Caribbean and areas such as Brazil, Belize, and Louisiana.

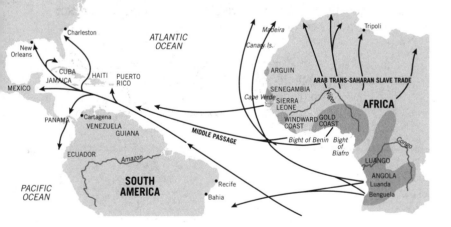

Hindu-Buddhist Religions ❶

Hinduism

- Who: South Asians and some Southeast Asians
- When: Earliest forms 7,500 years before present.
- Where: Mainly India; also today Bali in Indonesia, London, Manchester, and other parts of the former British Empire, with significant populations in Guyana, Trinidad, Fiji, Malaysia, and South Africa
- Scripture: Vedas, Upanishads, Bhagavad Gita, and other early Sanskrit texts
- Doctrine: The main personal practice is to work continuously toward multiple reincarnations and eventually nirvana. Practice of temple-based worship and festivals to praise particular supreme gods, including humanistic forms Vishnu, Shiva, Krishna, and animal forms Ganesha (elephant god) and Naga (serpent gods).
- Denominations: Different denominations are often based upon cults to deities. Based upon a hierarchical **caste system,** which is based upon the reincarnation principle, in which people are born into a particular social level where they remain for the rest of their lives.
- Historical Diffusion: **Expansion diffusion** from the Hindu hearth in Northern India. Later relocation diffusion across the Bay of Bengal to Southeast Asia (consider the historical Hindu temple complex at Angkor Wat in Cambodia) and to Indonesia where a remnant population is found today on the island of Bali.

The Caste System in India

The Hindu scriptures describe a **cosmology** (a belief in the structure of universe) in which there are several levels of existence, from the lowest animal forms to human forms and then higher animal forms, which are considered sacred, such as cattle, elephants, and snakes. The levels are known as **chakras.** As a soul is reincarnated it can be elevated to a higher *chakra,* if the soul has a positive karmic balance.

Once someone is born into a caste, he remains there for the rest of his life, no matter how rich or poor he becomes. The lowest human forms, *dalits* (often referred to as the "untouchables") are considered less holy due to their distance from nirvana on the *chakras*, whereas the Brahmins, the highest human form, are considered the priesthood of Hindus due to their relatively close position to the enlightened. Here are the five levels, or *varna,* within the human *chakra* that define the caste system in Hinduism:

BHRAMIN
Preists,
Academics

KSHATRIYA
Warriors, Kings

VAISHYA
Mechants, Landowners

SUDRA
Commoners, Peasants, Servants

DALITS
Outcast—Out of Caste. Street sweepers, latrine cleaners

Jainism

- Who: A fundamentalist interpretation of Hinduism
- When: Around 2,900 years before present
- Where: Western India
- Scripture: Texts collectively known as **Agamas.**
- Doctrine: At the core of religious practice is the complete respect for all other animal life, in that every living soul is potentially a divine god. Followers are strict vegetarians and often wear face masks to prevent the inhalation of insects.
- Denominations: Three main groups exist that differ in practice and worship.

- Historical Diffusion: Some Jain communities relocated to places such as Great Britain during the colonial period, 1830s to 1940s.

Buddhism

- Who: An ideological following that rejected the caste system and other Hindu practices.
- When: About 2,500 years before present
- Where: Hearth in the Gangetic Plain of North Central India and spread through Asia.
- Scripture: Early Hindu texts combined with the Tipitaka (*Pali Canon*), part of which contains the life and teachings of Siddhartha Gautama, the founder of Buddhism.
- Doctrine: A main doctrinal difference with Hinduism is the belief that nirvana can be achieved in a single lifetime with intensive study, meditation, and moral thought. Buddhism rejects the Hindu caste system as incompatible with the Buddhist view of human suffering.

- Denominations: Three traditions: Tibetan (Vajrayana); Southeast Asian (Theravada); and East Asian (Mahayana). Generally, Tibetan Buddhists are universalizing, accepting westerners into their community but uncompromising in their beliefs, while Theravada are less universalizing and do not compromise their traditions, and Mahayana are both universalizing and compromising.

- Historical Diffusion: Examples of Buddhism relocating across physical barriers: Tibetan Buddhism across the Himalayas and Tarim Basin desert to Siberia and Mongolia; Theravada from Sri Lanka across the Bay of Bengal to Southeast Asia; and Mahayana across the Himalayas to Eastern China.

Arrows show the diffusion of Buddhism across the
Himalayas and the Bay of Bengal

Abrahamic Religions ❗

Judaism

- Who: Larger groups including European Ashkenazi Jews, Sephardic Jews from North Africa, and the Middle East and Native Israelis known as *Sabra*.
- When: Over 5,700 years before present.
- Where: Hearth in Israel. Largest communities in Europe, United States, and Canada, particularly the metropolitan area around New York City and other urban areas worldwide, such as London, Antwerp, Paris, Los Angeles, Toronto
- Scripture: Torah (includes several books of the Old Testament) and Talmud
- Doctrine: Varied. All groups atone for sins during Yom Kippur and Rosh Hashanah.
- Denominations: Orthodox, Conservative, Reform, and Reconstructionism
- Historical Diffusion: The Jewish Diaspora begins in 70 CE with the Roman destruction of the Temple in Jerusalem, when Jews were forced out to other parts of the Empire. The post-WWII era following the Nazi Holocaust marks the beginning of the Jews' movement to Israel from Europe. Conflicts in the 1950s and 1960s caused migrations from North Africa and the Middle East to Israel.

Christianity

- Who: Originates in the Roman Empire; officially recognized in 4th century CE

- When: Following begins around 30 CE; expansion outside the Mediterranean in 6th century.

- Where: Europe, the Americas, Sub-Saharan Africa, Philippines, Austronesia

- Scripture: The Bible, divided into an Old Testament, including a modification of the Torah and dictates like the Ten Commandments, and a New Testament, which depicts the messianic life of Jesus of Nazareth and the writings of his disciples and early followers.

- Doctrine: Typically involves communions and baptisms, but depends on the denomination.

- Denominations: Eastern Orthodox, Armenian, Antiochian, Greek Orthodox, Coptic, Roman Catholic, Protestant; each can be subdivided into further practices and baptisms.

- Historical Diffusion: From the Mediterranean hearth, Christianity **diffused hierarchically** to large cities such as Rome, Constantinople, Alexandria, and Marseilles. From there missionaries spread the religion to other towns and cities where it diffused to smaller communities. These patterns of diffusion become recognizable through the hierarchy of the Holy See, archbishoprics, bishoprics, and local parishes.

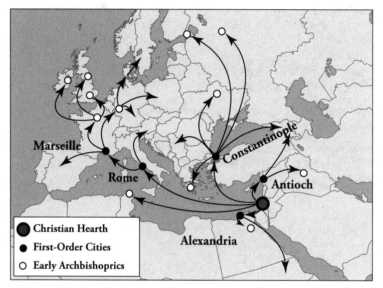

Islam

- Who: Origins on the Arabian Peninsula along the Red Sea; i.e., Mecca, Medina, and Jeddah
- When: Early 600s CE
- Where: Today the Islamic realm spans from Mauritania in West Africa, east to Indonesia and the Philippine Island of Mindanao; north to Chechnya, Kazakhstan, and Xinjiang in Western China; and south to Tanzania.

- Scripture: Koran (Quran), the scriptures received by Muhammad
- Doctrine: Pillars of Islam (at least five) and Haddith, the recorded sayings of Muhammad.
- Denominations: Sunni (85%) and Shia (15%) sects with a number of denominations within, such as the Ismaili Shiite and Wahabi Sunni. Shiites believe Imams (religious leaders) must have a direct bloodline to Muhammad.
- Historical Diffusion: As shown on the right, Islam diffused in an expansion pattern in all directions from Mecca very quickly. By 700 CE all of the Middle East and much of North Africa was adherent to Islam, with expansion into Europe and Asia happening through to the 1600s. Relocation diffusion was seen, such as that to Indonesia in the 1200s.

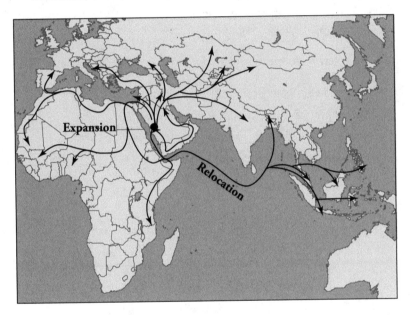

Islamic States: Theocractic, *Sharia,* and Secular Governance

Some Middle-Eastern countries are **theocracies,** where religious leaders hold the senior positions of governance. For example, Iran has a supreme religious council that serves as the **head of state** and can overrule the elected parliament and president. Furthermore, some Middle-Eastern countries are **republics or monarchies** that abide by *Sharia,* or Islamic law, based on the Koran and Haddith. A few absolute monarchies have all-powerful kings and large aristocracies who enforce religious standards on the populace.

Other Middle-Eastern states are more **secular,** meaning the state is not directly governed in a religious manner and often utilizes a French or British legal tradition and government structure. However, the influence of religion on government policy remains, leading to some **mixed-system** states, and tension between the secular government and religious activists can cause difficulty or violent conflict.

Here are a few Middle-Eastern examples of the aforementioned:

- Theocracies: Afghanistan, Iran, Saudi Arabia, and Yemen
- *Sharia* Law: Iran, Iraq, Saudi Arabia, and Sudan
- Secular: Azerbaijan and Turkey
- Mixed-System: Egypt, Jordan, and Oman

Moral Principles: The Five Pillars of Islam ❗

The Judeo-Christian system has its Ten Commandments from the Book of Exodus, which serves as a basic moral code for all followers. Likewise, the Koran emphasizes five pillars that guide followers with a moral system. The **five pillars of Islam** are as follows:

Five Daily Prayers	Islamic Creed	Alms to the Poor	Observance of Ramadan	The Hajj
• The call to prayer is broadcast throughout the Muslim world, at which point all work stops and prayer mats are laid out. • Prayer is done facing Mecca.	• Monotheistic creed: "There is only one god, Allah, & Muhammad is his prophet." • Muslims believe in some prophets from Judeo-Christian tradition, but Muhammad is the supreme prophet.	• All Muslims have a duty to care for and donate to the poor and sick. • Charitable foundations in the Islamic world help alleviate poverty, extend health care, and educate children.	• Ramadan, which is set on a lunar calendar, is a period of spiritual cleansing & repentance for past sins. • Fasting during daylight hours and meals after sundown.	• Each able Muslim must make at least one pilgrimage to Mecca during his lifetime. • "Haji" is an honorific name for those who make the journey. • Ramadan is the most popular time for the Hajj.

Syncretic Religions

Syncretic religions synthesize the core beliefs from two or more other religions. Examples of these include the **Druze,** who incorporate both Christian and Islamic principles, and the **Sikhs,** who incorporate principles from both Islam and Hinduism. Like Buddhists, Sikhs reject the concept of a caste-based social hierarchy.

Cultural Identity: Ethnicity and Race ❗

Cultural Identity, or the way people are identified and how they identify themselves, is another important aspect of cultural geography. A nation, in its most basic definition, is a population represented by a singular culture. Another term for nation would be a culture group. What defines a nation is a common identity, which is a complex of genetic heritage and political allegiance embodied in the term ethnicity. Ethnic groups often claim a single identifiable lineage or heritage, which all members tend to identify with as a common social bond. Keep in mind, as with our prior example of the English language, several ethnicities can exist within the same linguistic region. Likewise, within a single ethnicity more than one language can be used, such as the French Canadians, South Asian Indians, or Belgians.

Not all nations have a representative state, as a state in its most simple form is a population represented by a single government. This is the case with the example of the Gypsies, Roma, or Romani peoples of Europe and the Kurds of northern Iraq, southeastern Turkey, northeastern Syria, and western Iran. Ethnicity can be modified in the process of migration. In the United States and Canada, there are many migrant groups, including Italian-Americans and Irish-Canadians. This modified ethnicity is more than symbolic, and can be evidence of acculturation by immigrants to culture in their new home country.

Race !

Ethnicity and race are two commonly confused cultural identifiers. Whereas **ethnicity** represents the national heritage of an individual, **race** refers to the physical characteristics of a common genetic heritage. The concept of race was developed by physical anthropologists in the 1800s. Researchers categorized racial groups based on a number of variables including skin color, bone structure, and the shape of the hair shafts (straight, wavy, or curly). Keep in mind that over time these formerly scientific ideas were used crudely as the basis for racism within society and have lead to oppression, suffering, and war throughout the world. For many parts the world, identity is based on a single race being the **indigenous population**—the people who originally settled an area.

Three large, distinct racial groups emerged from this research:

- the Mongoloid or **Asiatic,** with a tan or yellowish skin tone, small body structure, and straight hair shaft;
- the Caucasian or **Indo-European,** with a light to dark skin tone, medium body type, and wavy hair shaft;
- the Negroid or **African,** with a dark skin tone, medium body shape, and a curly hair shaft.

Influence of Globalization on Cultural Change 🔰

Negative Effects of Globalization 🔰

Cultural globalization can harm indigenous cultures and threaten the constitution of national cultures. Influences such as literature, music, motion pictures, the Internet, and television (mainly from English-language sources) can diminish and potentially eliminate the media and culture of other linguistic groups.

The problem with cultural globalization is that when people are fully immersed in globalized popular culture, they are denying the importance of their own ethnic culture. Over time, unique and socially important traditions can be forgotten and lost.

Combating Cultural Globalization 🔰

To combat the negative effects of cultural globalization, some national governments around the world have instituted laws and regulations that lessen the impact of foreign influence on their home cultures. These laws and regulations can restrict certain types or limit the volume of foreign media and other external cultural influences. At times there are attempts to completely ban external cultural influence.

GLOBALIZATION EXPLAINED

Immigration and Emigration ⓘ

Migration is common and can take several different forms. **Interregional** or **internal migrants** move from one region of the country to another. This is the case with rural-to-urban migrants, who move from farm-land to cities within the same country, and intraregional migrants, who move from one area to another within the same region. There are also variations within international migration. **Transnational migration** occurs when migrants move from one country to another.

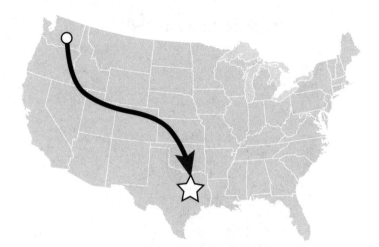

Internal Migration

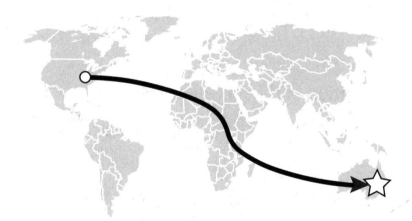

Transnational Migration

ASAP Human Geography

Human Capital Theory 🔊

Humans move for many reasons and there are several theories to explain the practice of migration, both between countries and internally. On the international side, the **human capital theory of migration** contends that humans take their education, job skills, training, and language skills (a.k.a. **human capital**) to a country where they can make more money and reap a higher net return. Higher levels of human capital (education, training, language skills) increase the expected net gain from migration. This flow of human capital from one country to another causes wages to fall in the destination country while pushing wages up in the sending country. Migration between the two countries stops only when the individual expected net earnings and costs of migration are the same.

Remittances 🔊

The receiving countries benefit from the flow of cheap labor into their economies. The socioeconomic cost of receiving this flow of immigrants includes crime, unemployment, and national security concerns. The largest positive economic effect of migration is the sending of remittances. Remittances are monetary and other cash transfers sent from transnational migrants to their families and communities back home. Often, more money flows back home in the form of remittances than the sending country receives in official development assistance. In rural Mexico, hundreds of communities are supported purely by the remittances of transnational labor migrants of their communities working in the United States.

Imperialism and Colonialism ⚠

Some of the greatest cultural change has been due to imperialism and colonialism. **Imperialism** can be thought of as the formal or informal political, military, or economic control a country exerts over another country. Closely related is **colonialism,** which occurs when a powerful nation either maintains or extends its control over other countries. Typically, a powerful nation colonizes (or creates settlements) in order to both extend their policies and exploit available resources. The significant difference between imperialism and colonialism is that the former refers to ideas, while the latter refers to the implementation of these ideas; i.e., colonies are the physical embodiment of imperialistic ideas.

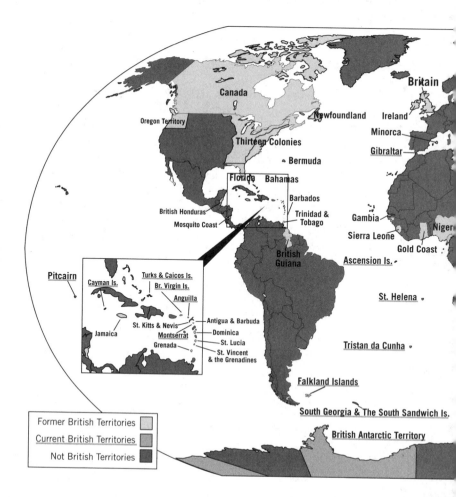

Have you ever heard the phrase, "the empire on which the sun never sets"? You have probably heard that saying used about the British Empire, but in fact it was originally used for the Spanish Empire (16th and 17th centuries). It's a saying that is used to describe certain global empires that were so extensive that there was always at least one part of their territory that was in daylight. The map below shows an assortment of nations that were once British territories and nations that are currently British territories and you can see why it was once used—they had a whole lotta territories!

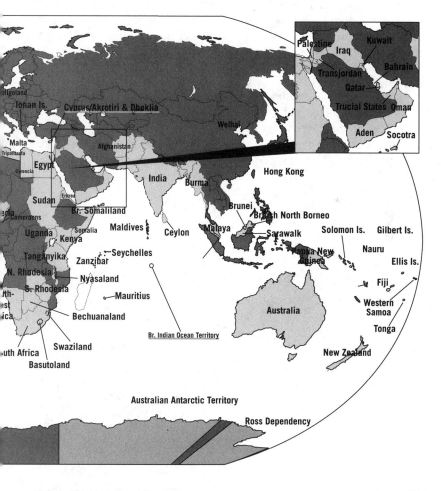

Cultural Identity and Environmental Determinism 🛈

The things that we see and hear in a culture form the cultural landscape. We can think about the cultural landscape as a form of **text** that can be read and we can read them to understand that place's cultural background and heritage. This takes a keen eye to see, and it helps to know some history of the place to translate what you are seeing. Each component of culture is expressed in a multitude of ways that signify and symbolize cultural influences. These historical influences can be as simple as the language used on a street sign or as complex as the cooking methods and spice mix in Louisiana Cajun food. Things are original to a single culture, but most things in the cultural landscape are the product of **cultural synthesis** or the blending together of two or more cultural influences. How people express their identity is dependent on the audience with which they are communicating—one can either express their **internal identity** or their **external identity.**

Internal Identity

- **Internal identity** is used by individuals to express their cultural heritage, ethnicity, or place of origin **to people who share** their heritage or place of origin.

External Identity

- **External identity** is used by individuals to express their cultural heritage, ethnicity, or place of origin **to people who do not share** a common cultural or geographic background.

You remember what it was like growing up in our hometown—during high school everybody would drive to the local gas station and hang out in the parking lot. Our parents thought we were crazy!

Let me tell you about my hometown—it was in a pretty rural area, so there wasn't much to do at night during high school. It might sound crazy, but we mostly drove to the local gas station parking lot to socialize.

Environmental Determinism and Racism !

In the 1800s, human geographers developed the concept of environmental determinism to explain cultural differences around the world. **Environmental determinism** is the former scientific ideology that states that a culture's traits are defined by the physical geography of its native hearth or culture region. Contemporary human geography as a science was originally based on deterministic philosophies. The *Anthropogeographie* of the German geographer **Friedrich Ratzel,** considered the father of modern human geography, and his students such as American Ellen Churchill Semple, built a large body of research claiming that all aspects of culture were defined by physical geographic factors such as climate, landforms, mineral resources, timber, food, and water supplies. The problem with environmental determinism was that science was being used to reinforce the racist ideologies of the 1800s and early 1900s.

Chapter 3 Key Terms

culture
culture group
nation
cultural landscape
signs, symbols
components of culture
cultural synthesis, syncretism
built environment
architectural forms
modern, contemporary
 architecture
traditional architecture
postmodern
commercial buildings
folk house
traditional housing style
New England, Cape Cod style,
 Saltbox
Federalist, Georgian style
I-House
relocation diffusion
stupa
pagoda
minaret
Wailing wall
official language
monolingual
multilingual
bilingual
linguistic region
language families
language groups
language subfamilies
prehistoric migrations
hearth
Anatolian theory
Hellespont
Kurgan theory
Eurasian steppe

English
lingua franca
linguistic region
dialect
word sounds, vocabulary
received pronunciation
Cockney
slang
pidgin
French Creole
patois
syncretic language
diffuse
indigenous
indigenous culture
preservation of cultural heritage
sequent occupancy
cultural adaptation
acculturation
assimilation
religion, belief systems
universalizing religions
ethnic religions
scripture
divine origin
doctrine
denominations
compromising religions
fundamentalists
polytheistic
monotheistic
migration diffusion
caste system
cosmology
Chakras
Agamas
theocracies
head of state
republics, monarchies

Chapter 3 Key Terms

Sharia
secular
mixed-system
Five Pillars of Islam
syncretic Religions
cultural identity
ethnicity
race
indigenous population
Asiatic
Indo-European
African

cultural globalization
interregional, internal migrant
transnational migration
human capital theory of migration
human capital
imperialism
colonialism
cultural synthesis
internal identity
external identity
environmental determinism
Friedrich Ratzel

CHAPTER 4

Political Organizations of Space

Citizens and space are inherently political and the borders between political states and political sub-unit areas (counties, parishes, districts, states, city limits) are finite lines. Political boundaries, as expressions of political control, must be definable and clear. Sometimes the physical geography (such as rivers or other bodies of water), defines boundaries and sometimes border lines are measured surveys based on treaties or other agreements between states. In this chapter we will think about the contemporary political map and where it came from.

The Contemporary Political Map ❶

There are a number of political geography terms such as nation and state that we use in everyday speech as synonyms. However, the technical definitions of terms have specific and important meaning in the geography of politics. Here's how to keep them straight:

Types of Political Entities ❶

- **Nation**: A population with a single culture. It's not a legal boundary.
- **State**: A population under a single government. It *is* a legal boundary.
- **Country**: An identifiable land area. It's not a legal boundary.
- **Nation-state:** A single culture under a single government whose population possesses a substantial degree of cultural homogeneity and unity.

Here are some fresh, hot examples to keep in mind:

Nations	State Name	Country
England, Scotland, Wales, Northern Ireland, Isle of Man, and the Channel Islands	United Kingdom of Great Britain and Northern Ireland	Great Britain or the British Isles
Han, Manchu, Zhuang, Miao, Uygur, Tibetan, and others	People's Republic of China	China
Anglo-Canadian, Québécois, and First Nations	Canada (former name Dominion of Canada)	Canada
French, German, Italian, and Romansch	*Confoederatio Helvetica* (in Latin)	Switzerland (French: *Suisse*) (German: *Schweiz*)

A nation-state is a single culture under a single government. Think Iceland or Argentina. But don't think Mongolia—the people are part Kazakh.

Ask Yourself...

America or the United States? Which one is a nation? Which one is a state? Which one is a country?

Stateless Nation, Multinational State, or Multistate Nation? !

All three of the following definitions use the words "nation" and "state," but they are totally different terms. Pay close attention!

Stateless Nation: A culture group that is not included or allowed to share in the political process. Examples: Kurds (ethnic group spread across northern and western Iraq, eastern Syria, and southeastern Turkey), Gypsies (Roma or Romani), Basques (ethnic group found in northern Spain, southwestern France).

Multinational State: A sovereign state which is viewed as composed of two or more nations. Examples: Czechoslovakia (split into Czech Republic and Slovakia in the 1990s). Yugoslavia (exploded in a fierce civil war during that same era, resulting in six different states—Bosnia and Herzgovina, Serbia, Croatia, Slovenia, the republic of Macedonia, and Montenegro).

Multistate Nation: A group of people with a shared ethnic or linguistic culture that resides in multiple states. Example: North and South Korea.

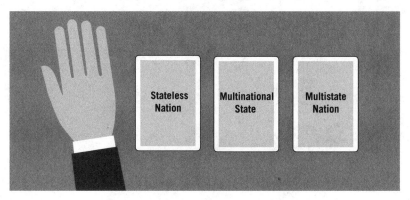

It's like a game of Three Card Monte.

Yo Dawg: An **autonomous region** is a subdivision or dependent territory of a country that has a degree of self-governance, or autonomy, from an external authority. In other words, it's almost a country within a country. Check out these examples of autonomous regions:

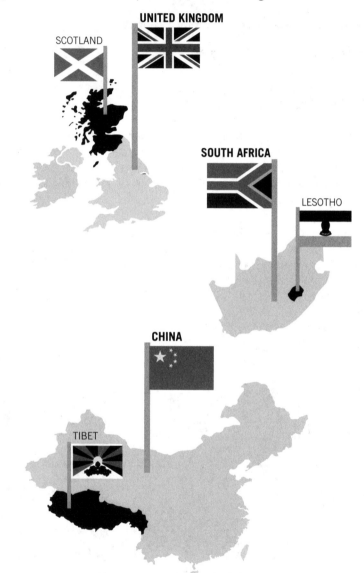

 Just like on *Pimp My Ride* when host Xzibit would hone in on the participant's hobbies so much that it felt like he was saying, "yo dawg, I heard you like to drive so we put a car in your car so you can drive while you drive."

114   ASAP Human Geography

Did You Know?

The world's smallest microstate, the Vatican City, has only 842 residents and measures .17 square miles.

Concept of Modern Nation-State

A **modern nation-state** is defined as a state in which the political entity is joined to the cultural and ethnic entity. In the past, the two have sometimes been separate. In more recent decades, other characteristics have come to include an effective political apparatus and a dynamic economy.

Example: Brazil. It's a vast country, the fifth-largest in the world in both area and population. It houses an enormous number of different types of cultures—indigenous tribes, descendants of African slaves, Portuguese, Germans, Japanese, and more. Nonetheless, the country has a national history, a national identity, and a national sport. The effectiveness of the Brazilian government varies from administration to administration, but is generally positive, and the Brazilian economy is one of the most powerful in the world.

Proponents of globalization have noted that the modern nation-state may become outmoded, replaced by a world government and a resurgence of ethnic tribalism.

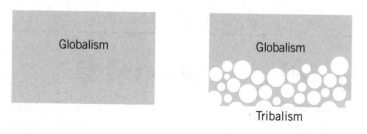

Current Nation State **Future Nation State**

The Impact of Colonialism ❗

Modern African nations, particularly south of the Sahara, were formed over a century ago at the **Conference of Berlin.** European colonial powers decided, with little input from the natives themselves, how the map of Africa would be drawn. As long as those European countries held power—the Dutch in South Africa, the French in Sierra Leone, the Portuguese in Angola—the boundaries held.

The problem? After World War II, most of those European countries divested themselves of their African colonies. And the native peoples, who remained loyal only to their tribe, found themselves politically grouped together with neighboring tribes, many of which had centuries of conflict. This is the reason for the genocide in Rwanda in the 1990s.

This is what is called **The Tyranny of the Map.**

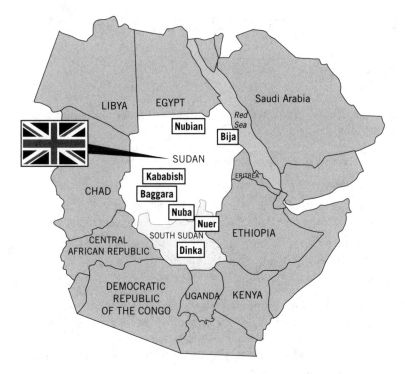

Sudan was a British colony from 1896–1955. The names of local tribes in Sudan are listed in boxes above.

Geopolitical Influences on Contempoary Political Map ~

Post-WWII

The fallout after World War II lead to major border shifts and changes in territorial boundaries:

- the boundary between Italy and France was modified
- the borders of Poland were redrawn
- the boundary between Poland and the Soviet Union (the Curzon Line confirmed at the 1945 Yalta Conference) was locked in
- Germany was split into four occupation zones and then was divided in two (East Germany, West Germany)
- and that's only a handful!

In addition, Western European colonial empires in Asia and Africa all collapsed (also known as decolonization) in the years after 1945. This left us with the contemporary political map. However, if there's one constant in this world—other than death and taxes—it's that boundaries will always be changing.

In this era, the United States and the Soviet Union became **superpowers.** They were friendly during WWII when they were unified as the Allies (along with Britain and China, of course), but they had very different worldviews and neither superpower wanted the other to peddle its influence and systems of government out to other nations.

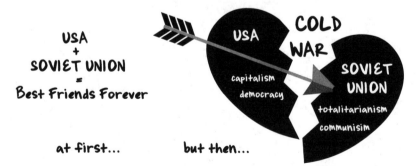

Fall of Communism 〰

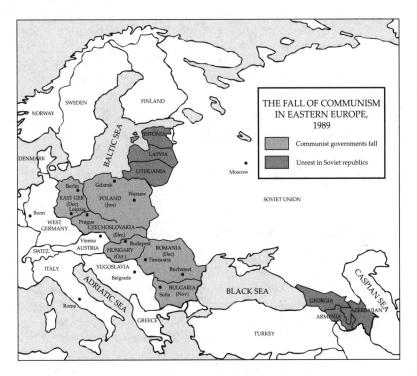

The Fall of Communism in Eastern Europe

Communist-led regimes collapsed in Hungary, Czechoslovakia, Bulgaria, Albania in 1989 and it was the beginning of the end of Communist rule in Eastern Europe. The Soviet Union, formerly a communist super-power, ended its rein with that title in 1991 when Mikhail Gorbachev's policies led to the dissolution of the union. Former Soviet Republics regained their independence and every school in the world had to buy a new map. Nations and borders were shifting all over in that era with East and West Germany becoming one, unified Germany in late 1989 (thanks to the Berlin Wall being toppled and after which David Hassel-hoff performed ON the wall and no, we are NOT kidding).

Don't Hassle the Hoff and don't doubt the German people's love of the former *Baywatch* star.

Political Organizations of Space

Do you know what the Heartland-Rimland Model is? The Shatterbelt Theory? These items won't necessarily be on the AP Human Geo exam, but you may wish to familiarize yourself with these concepts just in case (or to knock it out of the park and name drop these as cultural context in an essay).

Territorial Dimensions of Politics

Concept of Political Power

Political power isn't as fixed as we'd like to believe. In western-style democracies, actual power is partly based on the *perception* of power. If a leader *appears* to spend too much of that power unwisely, he or she loses all of it. Imagine a bank that steals all your remaining money if you dip below a certain threshold in your account. It's not always fair, but that's the situation described by the term **lame-duck president.**

Furthermore, even in this digital era, political power still congregates in physical places, the same way that religious power is concentrated in the Vatican City or economic power is concentrated in San Francisco. These are called **seats of government.** For example, Austin is the seat of government of the state of Texas; Bogotá is the seat of government of the nation of Colombia.

In the United States, seats of government come in three flavors: **local**, **state**, and **national**.

This explains the three layers of taxes that workers must pay. Most countries in the world have a similar triple layer of power, though sometimes under different names. In England, the local political body is called a **parish,** and in Canada a state is called a **province.**

 Did You Know?

In the United States, a *county* is a rural jurisdiction, and a *city* is an urban jurisdiction. However, these two jurisdictions often overlap, which creates confusion. The cit of Chicago, for example, resides within Cook County. Think of all the police procedural programs showing the turf wars between the sheriff's deputies and the city cops. (And sometimes even the FBI, too!)

Concept of Territoriality ❗

Territoriality is the effort to control pieces of Earth's surface for personal, political, or social ends. It's a community's sense of property and attachment toward its territory, as expressed by its determination to keep it inviolable and strongly defended.

Territoriality is the most basic form of power. The most elemental territoriality is personal space. European personal space is much smaller than American personal space, on average. Owned space is territory we claim because of legal ownership. Political space is territory that we claim to own because of political agreements.

Personal Space	Owned Space	Political Space
• People native to U.S., U.K., Nordic countries have need for great personal space • People native to Mediterranean countries tend to need significantly less	• a person's locker • a person's car • a person's house • a private high school	• a local police station • a public high school • The National Mall • The White House

---

 Did You Know?

In Slovenia, strangers keep a distance of almost three meters!

ASAP Human Geography

Nature and Function of Boundaries 🛑

- **Internal** boundaries are a type of boundary within a state (a nation state, that is), made for administrative purposes or to mark off cultural regions. The border between Los Angeles County and Orange County is a good example of an internal boundary.
- **International** boundaries exist between different nations. The border between North Korea and South Korea, known as the **Korean Demilitarized Zone,** is an example of an international border. Ironically, it's also the most militarized border on the planet!

NICE BOUNDARIES, BELGIUM!

This map displays international boundaries (the barrier between France and Belgium, Belgium and Luxembourg, Belgium and the Netherlands) and also internal boundaries (the barrier that determines the edge of Brussels or Antwerp, for example). Earlier in the chapter we talked about the idea of a nation or a nation state—Belgium is a sovereign state and is officially bilingual (French and Dutch).

Influence of Boundaries 🚩

On Identity

Boundaries influence people's identities. Think of the famous old saying that someone is "from the wrong side of the tracks." To an extent, a person's identity is formed largely by where he or she grew up. In some cultures, a person's neighborhood matters much more than others. The United States places less weight upon a person's place of origin than others countries do, since its culture is so individualistic. In European countries such as France, where class ascension is quite difficult, a person's hometown is extremely important in how he or she is perceived by peers.

On Interaction

When boundaries are agreed upon, all is peaceful. However, inevitably there are disputes. Here are four types of **boundary disputes**.

	What is it?	Example
Definitional	• border treaties are interpreted two different ways by states	Russian-Japanese Kuril Islands under Soviet control in 1945
Locational	• when the border moves, usually through natural events such as a river drying up	India-Bangladesh territory along the Ganges-Brahmaputra River
Operational	• when borders are agreed to, but passage across the border is a problem	New passport requirements for entry into the United States as a result of the Trump presidency
Allocational	• when a resource lies on both sides of a border	Disagreement between Mexico and the U.S. about the allocation of water from the Colorado River

Big Idea

For decades, the developed world has been creating a world with much weaker borders. Free trade has been the agreed-upon policy, with tariffs being mostly nonexistent. Open immigration policies have been in place as well. Currently, however, Europe and America are experiencing an equal but opposite reaction—the right-wing nationalist movement toward stronger borders. This so-called "alt-right" movement champions domestic manufacturing, tariffs on imports, intense nationalism, trade wars, and strict immigration policies. Time will tell if the movement toward a borderless world continues among developed countries.

Law of the Sea ❗

A 1982 United Nations Conference on the Law of the Seas (UNCLOS) proposed a clearer definition of the borders at sea.

Territorial Sea	First 12 miles out into the sea from the edge of the land is considered sovereign territory. All laws of that country apply.
Exclusive Economic Zone (EEZ)	For 200 miles, the country has exclusive economic rights to all resources, including fish, oil, gas, minerals, and salvage operations.
High Seas	Beyond 200 miles, no law of any country applies. Open fishing, gambling, marriages, divorces. Captains have power of law and can make arrests. If you've ever heard about mayhem erupting on a cruise ship, it was probably on the high seas.

Feast your eyes on these boundaries:

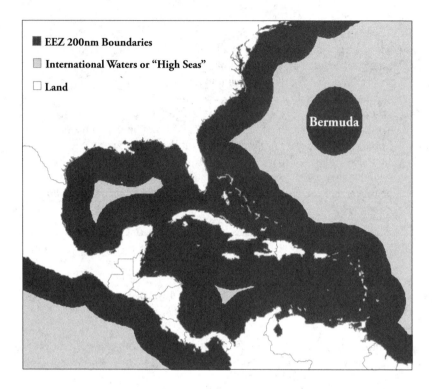

EEZ 200nm Boundaries

International Waters or "High Seas"

☐ **Land**

Bermuda

Forms of Governance

Unitary State Versus Federal State

In a **unitary state,** the power is held by one national (federal) government. Any administrative divisions that exist only have the powers that the central state delegates to them. This style of government effects change quickly but is also vulnerable to abuse. A classic example of a unitary state would be France under Louis XIV, who stripped power from the nobles by luring them to Versailles and turning them into nothing more than glorified courtiers.

In a **federal state**, the power is shared by a national (federal) and local (state) government. Conflict between the two governments is inevitable, and changes come more slowly, but abuse is more easily prevented with such a balance. Example: The United States of America where powers are shared between the federal government and the state government.

Territorial Morphology ❗

The shape of a country is often what helps to identify it on a map. To some degree, the shape of a country or state also impacts its society and external relations with other countries and states. Here is a run-down of major types of state/country morphology (shape):

Type	Description	Example
Compact	Shape without irregularity	POLAND
Fragmented	Broken into pieces; archipelagos	The Florida Keys
Elongated	Appears stretched-out, long	VIETNAM
Prorupt	Has a panhandle or peninsula	ITALY

Perforated	Has a hole(s) (country, large lake)	Lake Okeechobee
Landlocked	Has no sea or ocean borders	Kansas

Some of these morphologies have cultural characteristics associated with them. For example, most landlocked states—from Kazakhstan to Kansas—often display suspicion of outsiders. The reason: For millennia, travelers only had one option—the sea. Without any ports, such landlocked areas saw virtually no travelers, and have historically remained less accustomed to outsiders.

 ### *Did You Know?*

Bhutan, an isolated and landlocked state in the Himalayas, charges travelers $250 per day to visit!

Challenges to Contemporary Political-Territorial Arrangements

In a purist view of the world, states exist as purely independent entities, arranged shoulder-to-shoulder across the planet. In this vision of human societies, states are like crystals—stable, perfect, and unchanging.

That, however, is not how the world looks. Let's look at two major challenges to this view of the world.

Challenge #1: Supranationalism

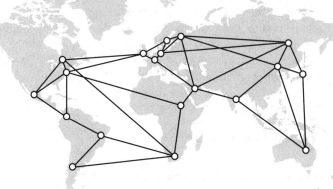

Supranationalism is the concept of two or more sovereign states allied together for a common purpose. Most of these agreements are formed for trade alliances, military cooperation, and diplomacy.

Historically, these agreements have been made for three different reasons:

1. **Economies of scale.** When the number of products increases, the cost of each item decreases. For example, producing 50 T-shirts for an improv comedy troupe is cheaper, per shirt, than producing only 5 T-shirts. There are economies of scale that come specifically with supranational agreements. Companies are free to pursue cheaper labor and resources in other countries. An American firm that hires people in India to staff its call center is a good example of an economy of scale aided by supranational agreements.

2. **Trade Agreements.** Most trade agreements are made to keep the flow of products moving smoothly between states. One of the oldest surviving trade agreements in Europe, for example, is the Methuen Treaty, signed in 1703. In it, the English agreed to place a smaller tariff on Portuguese wine than on French wine, and the Portuguese agreed to import English woolen cloth without any tariff at all.

3. **Military Alliances.** History is filled with examples of countries who agreed to come to one another's defense against a common enemy. That's how World War I started. History is also filled with military alliances formed to keep peace, such as the German-Soviet Non-Aggression Pact (which the Nazis broke).

 Did You Know?

One supranational agreement, the European Coal and Steel Community, eventually led to the creation of the entire European Union!

Multinational organizations are international bodies that serve a purpose ranging from economic to political to environmental to social justice. Some are governmental; others, non-governmental. The most famous include the **United Nations** and the **European Union.**

Additional Supranational Organizations	
Other Examples of Supranational Organizations	**Purpose**
North Atlantic Treaty Organization (NATO)	Military
Organization of Petroleum Exporting Countries (OPEC)	Oil Pricing Cartel
North American Free Trade Agreement (NAFTA)	Free-Trade Zone
Organization of African Union (OAU)	Regional Diplomacy
World Bank and International Monetary Fund (IMF)	Government Loans

Challenge #2: Devolution of States

Just as some states evolve and strengthen relationships, others devolve. This can mean movement from a national government to various regional governments within the state. It can also mean a large state breaking up into various independent states.

There are many forces that contribute to **devolution of states:**

Physical Geography	Regions on remote frontiers, mountainous terrain, isolated villages, and islands tend to demand separation from the central government. See Taiwan's relationship with China.
Ethnic Separation	In Rwanda, the old conflict between the Hutu tribe and the Tutsi tribe led to a genocide that nearly destroyed the society.
Terrorism	Planned violent attacks upon a state can weaken or destroy the state. Some are stateless groups such as Al Qaeda. Sometimes the terrorism is done by the government itself—in Cambodia, the leader of the Khmer Rouge, Pol Pot, killed one-quarter of the population.
Economic and Social Problems	The former Soviet Union was beset by economic problems—it couldn't spend enough to keep up with the U.S. on defense—and multicultural problems. Gorbachev loosened the iron grip, and the entire system fell apart.
Irredentism	An ethnic minority splits off from a larger multiethnic state. Chechnya has tried to break away from the Russian Federation, with mixed results.

In summary, supranationalism and devolution are almost perfect opposites, but they're exactly alike in one key respect—both serve to weaken the state as an independent entity (for better or worse).

Chapter 4 Key Terms

nation
state
country
nation-state
stateless nation
multinational state
multistate nation
autonomous region
modern nation-state
Conference of Berlin
tyranny of the map
superpowers
lame-duck president
seats of government
parish, province
territoriality
internal boundaries

international boundaries
The Demilitarized Zone
boundary disputes—definitional,
  locational, operational,
  allocational
territorial seas
Exclusive Economic Zone (EEZ)
high seas
unitary state
federal state
supranationalism
economics of scale
trade agreements
military alliances
United Nations
European Union
devolution of states

CHAPTER 5

Agricultural and Rural Land Use

Next let's explore the topics of agricultural and rural land use (then later in the book we'll head into the city and explore urban land use). This chapter will cover assorted agricultural revolutions and their resultant negative and positive effects, farming and crops, food production, settlement patterns, and more. Let's head out to the country!

First Agricultural Revolution
10,000 B.C.E.—2,000 B.C.E. ❗

Throughout history, **agricultural revolutions** are periods of time in which significant innovations in farming occur. Such innovations were important as they often reduced the amount of labor needed to produce goods and increased the amount of goods harvested per unit of land.

The **First Agricultural Revolution,** also known as the **Neolithic Revolution,** refers to the period of time when people transitioned from hunting and gathering for food, to an organized system of farming.

Keep in mind that this transition did not occur all at once. Instead, agriculture evolved in various geographic locations and successful processes diffused around the world over time.

Limitations of Diffusion

Growing areas of crops and livestock expanded as domesticated varieties were traded and diffused across the landscape. However, growing areas are limited by climate, weather, and culture.

Agricultural Innovations 💬

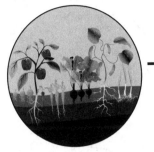

Vegetative planting, where shoots, stems, and roots of existing wild plants are collected and grown together, was the first phase of early farming.

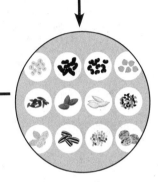

This led to **seed agriculture,** where fertilized seed grains and fruits of plants are collected and replanted together.

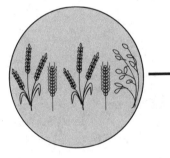

Over time, farmers reject poorly growing crops and took cuttings and seeds from productive, heartier crops to grow future generations. This **domestication of plants** led to early forms of **horticulture.**

Animal domestication, the process in which selected animal populations become accustomed to human provision and control, was established as an alternative to hunting and fishing.

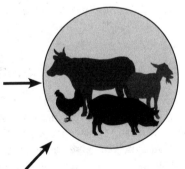

Productive breeds were purposely interbred or hybridized for reproduction through a process known as **animal husbandry.** The diffusion of animal hybrids was specialized by region.

Early Centers of Plant & Animal Domestication 💬

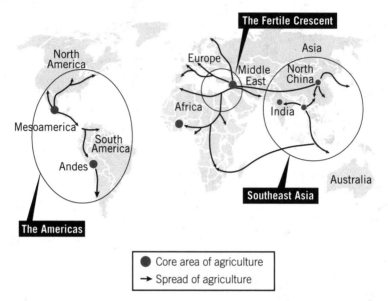

Among this map of early centers of plant and animal domestication is the "Fertile Crescent" which may be a new term to you. The Fertile Crescent is the nickname of a region in the Middle East that stretches from the Persian Gulf through regions that are now known as Iraq, Syria, Lebanon, Jordan, Israel, northern Egypt. It's known as the birthplace of agriculture, urbanization, writing, trade, science, history, and organized religion.

The Columbian Exchange 💬

With the conquest of mainland Central and South America in the early 1500s, a number of domesticated New World crops made their way to the rest of the world through **relocation diffusion.** We call this the **Columbian exchange,** as it is historically symbolized by diffusion that occurred after the voyages of Christopher Columbus. And by "diffusion" we mean the spreading of plants and animals from the New World to the Old World (via trade ships) and vice versa. Animals also diffused during this time, but mostly in the opposite direction of plants: Many Old World animals made their way to the New World. Explorers took animals to the New World and brought plants back with them.

New World to Old World		Old World to New World	
• Rubber trees	• Tobacco	• Olives	• Tea
• Turkeys	• Tomatoes	• Honey bees	• Oats
• Pumpkins	• Yams	• Oranges	• Barley
• Corn	• Parrots	• Bananas	• Chickens
• Avocados	• Beans	• Wheat	• Cows
• Strawberries	• Peppers	• Turnips	• Sheep
• Papayas	• Peanuts	• Lemons	• Horses
• Pineapple	• Potatoes	• Pears	

Second Agricultural Revolution
Late 1700s AD—Mid 1900s AD 🛑

The **Second Agricultural Revolution** came about from technological innovations in agriculture and manufacturing that drastically reduced labor requirements and increased the scale of farm production. This revolution introduced specialized **hybrid crops,** artificial **chemical fertilizers,** early **chemical pesticides,** and **mechanization. Tractors, combine harvesters,** and other mechanized foodprocessing devices made vast improvements in crop yields for farmers.

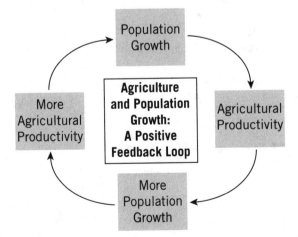

Advances from First Agricultural Revolution ❗

1.

Innovations in farming **technology,** such as devices like Eli Whitney's cotton gin (1793) and the McCormick reaper (1830s), reduced labor requirements and increased farm production. Such technological innovations, coupled with tractors and combine harvesters, improved both the quality and quantity of crop production.

2.

The 2nd agricultural revolution heralded massive advances in horticulture and chemistry. Scientific horticulture uses laboratory techniques to develop plant and animal hybrids that grow larger or under certain climatic conditions to meet the needs of farmers in different regions.

Dwarf varieties were an important plant hybrid innovation. Shorter breeds of both wheat and rice were found to be heartier and more productive because the plant spent less time and energy growing a stalk, resulting in more and larger grains on each head.

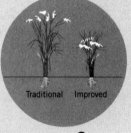

Traditional   Improved

3.

German chemists developed both artificial **fertilizers** and chemical **insecticides** such as ammonium nitrate, the first mass-produced as a fertilizer designed to replace lost nitrogen in soils. **Pesticides** were developed from natural sources and from synthetic chemicals. Developments included insecticides, fungicides, herbicides, rodenticides and nematicides, which kill harmful worms either in soils or within foods.

Impact of the 2nd Agricultural Revolution ⚠️

 The mechanization of agriculture led to a decreased need for labor and an increased dependence on machinery. While mechanization had a massive impact, such innovations did not diffuse to Third-World countries until much later.

 Small farms were no longer profitable, leading to the decline of individual farms and the rise of commercial farming. Not only did this lead to a decline in the number of individual farmers, but it also led to the rise of the large, industrial farm.

 Agricultural chemicals, hybridization, and large-scale highly mechanized farms have enabled the global population to expand from two billion to more than seven billion. Furthermore, average human life expectancy increased dramatically due to an improved diet resulting from increased access to quality, affordable food.

During industrialization in the 1800s and the early 1900s, there was a rapid rural-to-urban migration as agricultural work opportunities declined and manufacturing jobs increased.

Link to the Demographic Transition Model ∽

The 2nd Agricultural Revolution aligns with early stage three in the Demographic Transition Model. Stage three was achieved in Europe and the Americas during this revolution, but was not achieved in Third-World countries.

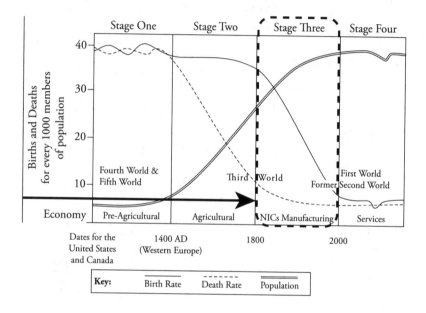

The Green Revolution !

The **Green Revolution,** which occurred in the 1950s and 1960s, was when increased technologies, pesticides, and fertilizers led to the development of higher-yield and faster growing crops. Such innovations allowed famers in the Third World to increase crop production on small plots of land.

The technology transfer from First to Third World also led to population growth in Third-World countries. Without expanded food production, the growing populations in the post–World War II developing world would have led to disastrous global food shortages, as opposed to periodic regional famines that occur due to drought or civil war.

+ Positive Effects

- Mechanization, fertilizers, and pesticides led to improved crop production on small plots of land and reduction in worldwide hunger

- Decreased price of food.

- Affordable mechanization means through **irrigation pumps,** which can be purchased at a low cost to move water to farming regions.

- **Genetic engineering** allowed farmers to modify crops with beneficial traits and create **high-yield seeds.**

- **Biotechnology** research that led to the development of vaccines, antibiotics, and growth hormones.

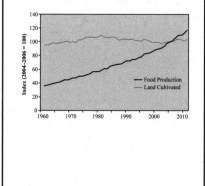

– Negative Effects

- Due to the high cost of large-scale farm equipment, mechanization has been slow to diffuse in Third-World countries.

- Small farms suffered as they were unable to capitalize on economies of scale, or when unit costs of production decrease while quantities produced increase.

- Detrimental environmental impact caused by the increased use of energy, materials, and machinery. Particularly, chemical use led to **eutrophication,** when fertilizer flows into bodies of water and floods the water with nutrients, that has caused explosive algae growth and water pollution.

- The use of fertilizers and pesticides has led to **pesticide resistance,** the process when pests evolve to have genetic resistance to a previously effective pest-control chemical.

- Fear and distrust of genetically modified plants and animals.

Agricultural Production Regions ❗

Modern commercial agriculture relies on a more inclusive way of farming and the internationalization of industrialized farming that we'll cover later in this chapter, but for now look into the way that climate conditions dictate the agricultural products of a given region.

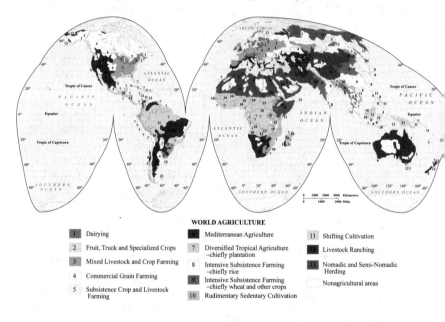

WORLD AGRICULTURE

1 Dairying	**6** Mediterranean Agriculture
2 Fruit, Truck and Specialized Crops	**7** Diversified Tropical Agriculture –chiefly plantation
3 Mixed Livestock and Crop Farming	**8** Intensive Subsistence Farming –chiefly rice
4 Commercial Grain Farming	**9** Intensive Subsistence Farming –chiefly wheat and other crops
5 Subsistence Crop and Livestock Farming	**10** Rudimentary Sedentary Cultivation

11 Shifting Cultivation
12 Livestock Ranching
13 Nomadic and Semi-Nomadic Herding
Nonagricultural areas

The trends in shading show a way that a region's method of agricultural production is directly linked to a region's climate!

Mediterranean Agriculture

The areas of Africa, Asia, and Europe that surround the Mediterranean Sea have a warm, dry climate with short periods of rain in winter and spring. In this region, the domestication of plants has specialized certain varieties of crops that today bring significant value to farmers. Here is a short list of **Mediterranean agriculture** crops that have been domesticated and continuously grown in the region: citrus, nuts, palms, olives, artichokes, avocadoes, and grapes. Other parts of the world with climates similar to the Mediterranean have also adopted these specialized crops. These places include Southern and Central California, Central Florida, South Texas, Southern and Central Brazil, Southern China and Southeast Asia, Hawaii, Northern Argentina, Uruguay, Central Chile, Black Sea Coastal Areas, South Africa, and Southern Australia.

Specialized Agriculture

In order to survive the fall of the family farm, many individuals started to produce **specialized farm products.** Unlike staple grain farming, specialized crops play an important role in the diversity of foods in terms of both farm economy and the cultural specificity of consumers. Specialized crops bring much higher amounts of money per acre than basic grain staples. While these farms tend to be smaller than grain farms, specialized crops can still be produced in large-scale operations. Be aware of the following examples of specialized agriculture for the AP Human Geography exam.

Natural Food

- Those resistant to **genetically modified organisms (GMOs),** skeptics of artificial hormones, and people concerned about **animal welfare** have rejected many of the farming practices used by agribusiness and other farmers. In turn, a large market for so-called **natural food products** has emerged. In most places, to be labeled **organic,** crops and animals must not be grown using genetic engineering, must be free of pesticides, antibiotics, and synthetic hormones, must not use artificial fertilizers, and must feed on completely organic crops.

Dairy

- **Dairying** is done mainly with cows but can also be a specialized agricultural activity using goats and buffalo for cheese production. Dairying is today a massive global operation that yields milk for drinking, cheeses, yogurt, butter, and cream. With the development of pasteurization, the amount of area that could be served by dairies expanded; the region around a city to which fresh milk is delivered without spoiling is known as the **milkshed.** Multiple large dairies are necessary to supply large cities. Processed dairy has continually moved westward over the last 150 years to "America's Dairyland," Wisconsin, and other parts of the upper Midwest.

Subsistence Agriculture

Intensive mixed farming that provides all of the food and material needs of a household is commonly called **subsistence agriculture.** A single farm can produce staple grain crops, fruits, and vegetables along with meat, eggs, milk, wool, and leather, having animals pull plows during planting and loads during harvest. This allows people to settle permanently and subsist without having to migrate seasonally. **Extensive subsistence agriculture** occurs when there are low amounts of labor inputs per unit of land.

Monoculture is the agricultural practice of cultivating a single crop or livestock species on a piece of land (remember that MONO is more than just the nickname of that sickness that everyone is scared of getting in their high school and college years—it means "one"). Monoculture became common in the era of early political civilizations, when farms produced a **staple crop** in large order to feed whole societies and armies.

Multi-cropping was more secure than monoculture. If one crop failed or was damaged, another crop would provide a backup food supply. Today, most subsistence agriculture is usually very intensive and done on small plots of land. In much of the Third World, the **physiologic density,** or number of people per unit of **arable land** (farmable land), is very high compared to the First World; i.e., more people have to be fed off of less land in the Third World.

Subsistence practices require farmers to have innate knowledge of plants, animals, soils, and climate and the ability to preserve foods for long-term consumption and for times of need. **Food preservation** via drying, pickling, cooking, and storage jars has been a necessity for survival for thousands of years.

As a result, many **specialized crops** were grown for both immediate consumption and preservation. For example, cabbages spiced with red pepper and soaked in vinegar were buried in clay storage jars to make kimchi in Korea starting eight thousand years ago. Likewise, cucumbers were grown in Eastern Europe and preserved in either lime or salt water to make pickles. Meats are preserved by drying, smoking, sugarcuring, or salting for long-term preservation.

Subsistence Agriculture & the Demographic Transition Model ❶

You can also relate agricultural practices to specific stages of the Demographic Transition Model. Historically, stage one of the model was characterized by pre-agricultural societies engaged in **subsistence farming** and **transhumance,** that is, the seasonal migration for food and resources or owning livestock. Based on current demographic data, there are no stage one countries in existence today. However, Third-World countries that engage in long periods of warfare exhibit late stage one characteristics.

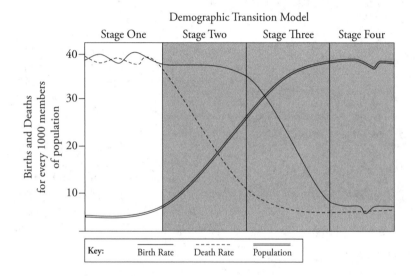

Demographic Transition Model

Commercial Agriculture

The opposite of intensive subsistence farming is **cash-cropping** to sell farm goods at market. This is a form of extensive agriculture in which harvested crops are exchanged for currency, goods, or credit. The credit is then used to buy equipment or seed for the next planting season and in part to buy food, clothing, and other necessities for the farm family. The **commercial crops** are transported, sold at other markets, and finally preserved or processed into other goods for sale. That describes small-scale cash-cropping, but large-scale corporate operations also engage in nonsubsistence farming. Modern commercial agriculture has radically changed the organization of farming. The dominant form today is **corporate agriculture,** or **agribusiness,** where large-scale extensive farms of several thousand acres or several thousand animals are controlled by a single regional business.

The Most Lucrative Food Crop by State (2012)	
WHEAT	Oregon, Nevada, Montana, Utah, Colorado, Noth Dakota, South Dakota, Nebraska, Kansas, Oklahoma, Texas, Minnesota, Iowa, Illinois, Missouri, Indiana, Michigan, Ohio, Kentucky, Noth Carolina, Virginia, Maryland, Delaware.
RICE	Arkansas, Mississippi
POTATOES	Idaho, Alaska, Maine, Wisconsin
APPLES	Washington, West Virginia, New Hampshire, New York
PEANUTS	South Carolina, Georgia, Alabama
SUGARCANE	Hawaii, Lousiana
ORANGES	Florida
GRAPES	California
MAPLE SYRUP	Vermont
MUSHROOMS	Pennsylvania
CRANBERRIES	Massachusetts
BLUEBERRIES	New Jersey
SWEET CORN	Rhode Island, Connecticut
PECANS	New Mexico
BEANS	Wyoming
LETTUCE	Arizona

Hallmarks of Modern Commercial Agriculture

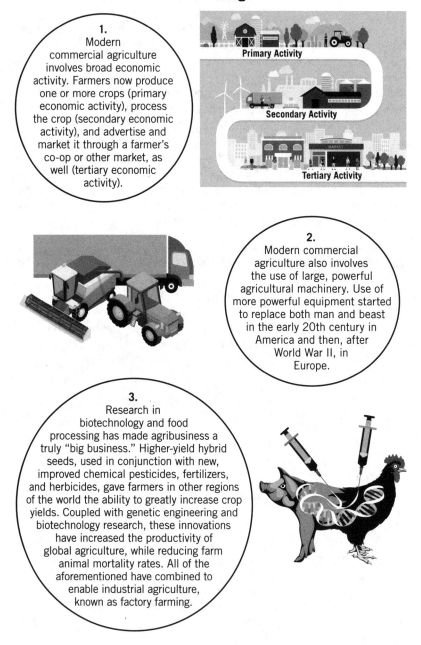

1. Modern commercial agriculture involves broad economic activity. Farmers now produce one or more crops (primary economic activity), process the crop (secondary economic activity), and advertise and market it through a farmer's co-op or other market, as well (tertiary economic activity).

Primary Activity
Secondary Activity
Tertiary Activity

2. Modern commercial agriculture also involves the use of large, powerful agricultural machinery. Use of more powerful equipment started to replace both man and beast in the early 20th century in America and then, after World War II, in Europe.

3. Research in biotechnology and food processing has made agribusiness a truly "big business." Higher-yield hybrid seeds, used in conjunction with new, improved chemical pesticides, fertilizers, and herbicides, gave farmers in other regions of the world the ability to greatly increase crop yields. Coupled with genetic engineering and biotechnology research, these innovations have increased the productivity of global agriculture, while reducing farm animal mortality rates. All of the aforementioned have combined to enable industrial agriculture, known as factory farming.

Family Farms, Agribusiness, and Complex Commodity Chains, Oh My!

Commodity chain analysis explains the links between producers and consumers in the production and distribution of a commodity. **Commodity chains** exist from the small-scale, family-based producers selling directly from the farm or through local farmers' markets to transnational supply networks selling to an international customer base.

Small-Scale, Farm-to-Consumer Commodity Chain

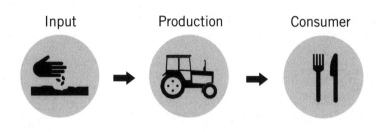

Input   Production   Consumer

 Did You Know?

LET'S TALK TEA: Tea production employs millions of people worldwide, and most of them live in remote, poverty-stricken communities. The tea supply chain is very intricate and involves many players. Tea leaves are grown either on large estates with their own processing factories or by thousands of small farmers, who send their tea leaves to a local factory. From there, the tea moves to a broker, who auctions it off to an international trader. The international trader sells the tea to various tea companies, who then sell the product to retailing and catering companies and the consumer finally gets the box of tea bags. In this long and detailed commodity chain, only a few powerful multinational companies control the buying and retailing of tea. Most of the profits are made at the retail end of tea's commodity chain and the oversupply of tea (combined with the poverty of the producers) is a matter of great concern to international aid groups.

Agribusiness Commodity Chain

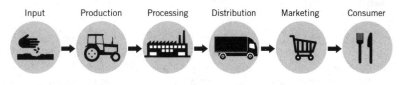

Input   Production   Processing   Distribution   Marketing   Consumer

Agribusiness & the Demise of the Family Farm

The traditional, small-scale family farm has faced difficult times because of a few factors:

- low crop prices
- low profitability
- increasing fuel costs
- competition from big agribusiness firms

Beginning in the 1970s, the United States and Canadian governments extended vast amounts of low-interest loans, price supports, and other subsidy programs to aid farmers who at the time had significant political influence in agricultural states and provinces. This was a necessary bailout of farms, which would have shut down without the public supply of credit to buy seed, chemicals, and equipment at the start of planting seasons. Most banks saw farms as risky creditors, and the government had to step in as a lender of last resort.

If the government hadn't bailed out farmers, a mass closure of farms would have led to wild price swings in food, and things were bad enough with fuel prices in the 1970s at then all-time highs. Many farms' mortgages were foreclosed due to the farmers' inability to make money as a result of low **commodity prices** for crops (the prices set by market traders at mercantile exchanges for volumes of crops like bushels of corn or pork bellies). Eventually agribusiness stepped in during the 1980s and 1990s, buying up and consolidating many farms into larger holdings. As a result, some farm communities nearly disappeared as people left to find a new life in other parts of the country.

Intensive & Extensive Land Use ⓧ

The type of labor and area of activity are used to classify agricultural activity. There are two main classifications:

- **intensive agriculture,** which requires many labor inputs, is focused on a small plot of land, or both
- **extensive agriculture,** which requires limited labor inputs, is spread across large areas of land, or both

Intensive Land Use

Early crop farmers added domesticated animals to their holdings, resulting in **mixed farming.** This is also referred to as **general farming,** where multiple crops and animals exist on a single farm to provide diverse nutritional intake and non-food items. Intensive mixed farming that provides for all of the food and material needs of a household is commonly called **subsistence agriculture.** (Remember that term from a few pages back?)

Market gardening is the small-scale production of flowers, fruits, and vegetables that are sold directly to local consumers. Labor is done manually, and involves growing a diverse set of crops on a small area of land over a single growing season.

Extensive Land Use

The domestication of herd animals led to **pastoralism,** or agriculture based on the seasonal movement of animals from winter to summer pastures and back again. This is known as **nomadic herding.**

Traditionally, **slash and burn agriculture** (also known as **swidden**) has occurred in tropical rainforest regions with farmers shifting from one plot of land to another every few years as soil nutrients become depleted; this is known as **shifting cultivation.** Land abandoned by farmers was allowed to **fallow,** and natural vegetation would return and increase the nutrient biomass of the area.

In the tropical and sub-tropical climates of the world, it is common to find extensive **plantation agriculture,** specialized crops intended for both **domestic consumption** and for export to other parts of the world.

Plantations tend to be large, extensive monoculture farms that are reliant upon low-wage labor and, historically in the United States until 1865, slave labor. Today, tropical plantation export crops are found mainly in Third-World locations. Some of the most common plantation crops are bananas, cane sugar, coffee, tea, rubber, cacao, and palm oil.

In the semi-arid climates of the world, extensive agricultural activity known as **livestock ranching** takes place over vast swaths of sparsely vegetated land with low soil quality. American livestock ranchers tend to focus on cows and chickens, while Chinese ranchers produce pigs.

Agricultural Activity & The Environment 💬

Let's start off with some key terms:

- **Human Ecology:** human interactions with nature
- **Human-Environment interactions:** forestry techniques, fisheries, environmental regulation, farming practices

Farming practices can be criticized for their dependence on external inputs such as fuel, agricultural chemicals like pesticides and fertilizers, and the effects of farming on soil erosion and local water usage. As soils become depleted and water becomes the earth's most precious commodity, protecting these resources has become a major movement.

The following are environmental problems associated with agricultural activity that you should know for the AP Human Geography Exam.

Overgrazing & Desertification

Extensive pastoralism, the shifting of animal herds between grazing pastures, has remained popular in several arid parts of the world (especially Africa, Middle East, Central Asia), where dry grassland is the common landcover. This problem is similar to that of rainforest destruction, since too many people and too many animals are placing **population pressure** on too little land. **Overgrazing** has led to significant amounts of dry grassland being denuded, eroded, and as a result, desertified. **Desertification** is any human process that turns a vegetated environment into a desert-like landscape. In addition to overgrazing, deforestation and **soil salinization** can also lead to desertification.

Irrigation Agriculture

The practice of **irrigation** opens up more land to cultivation than would normally be possible in arid climates. Irrigation agriculture is responsible for close to three-quarters of world freshwater use and up to 90% of freshwater use in the most povertystricken countries of the world. Governments often heavily subsidize irrigation agriculture and the crops produced are often worth less than the water. The Nile Valley in Egypt is an example of heavily subsidized irrigation agriculture. Unfortunately, the water for these irrigation farms comes from underground water tables called **aquifers.** These aquifers are being depleted at a rapid rate and large-scale grain-producing countries such as India, China, and the United States are examples of those caught in this predicament.

Deforestation

Deforestation is the act of clearing, generally by cutting down or burning, a forested area of trees and other vegetation without the intention of replanting. Not only does rainfall sap the remaining nutrients from the soil, but deforestation places pressure on a valuable, natural resource—oxygen—and lessens the earth's ability to filter CO_2.

Wetland Destruction

A **wetland** is an area of land that is covered in fresh water, salt water, or a combination of the two. Wetlands include marshes, ponds, deltas, and lake or ocean edges. Wetland destruction occurs when wetland areas are drained and filled for land that can be used for small-scale farming, agribusiness, or commercial developments.

Water Pollution

Right now, the biggest source of water pollution is agricultural activities. The particular sources that are responsible for water pollution are called **point sources,** and pollution that has many sources or no definitive source are **nonpoint sources.**

One continual problem that contributes to water pollution is that runoff from farmland carries excess nutrients and pollutants to streams. This can result in large **dead zones** (areas that don't support life), as standing bodies of water such as ponds, reservoirs, and lakes do not recover quickly from the addition of pollutants. The lack of water flow prevents the pollutants from being diluted, which means that they accumulate in the water and undergo **biomagnification** in the food chain. In a similar way, groundwater does not recover well from the addition of pollutants because, again, there is very little movement of water. Furthermore, groundwater is generally very cold and low in dissolved oxygen, which makes recovery from degradable waste a slow process.

Another problem that arises from the large number of grazing animals worldwide is the large amount of **animal waste** produced. Manure is not used as fertilizer due to difficulty with transport. It has instead become the most widespread source of water pollution in America.

Soil Degradation

One of the risks of farming in dryland and desert regions is that the evaporation of water can trap **mineral salts** on the surface soil layer. High daytime temperatures cause water vapor to be drawn out of irrigated farmland. As evaporation continues over several growing seasons, the amount of mineral salt can build to toxic levels and poison crops. The land has to be either abandoned or flooded by about 18 inches of fresh water over a couple of months to draw out the salts. Fresh water, though, tends to be expensive and in short supply in these dry areas.

Chapter 5 Key Terms

agricultural revolutions
First Agricultural Revolution
  (Neolithic Revolution)
growing areas
vegetative planting
seed agriculture
domestication of plants,
  horticulture
animal domestication
animal husbandry
relocation diffusion
Columbian exchange
Second Agricultural Revolution
hybrid crops
chemical fertilizers
chemical pesticides
mechanization
tractors
combine harvesters
technology
dwarf varieties
fertilizers
insecticides
pesticides
Green Revolution
irrigation pumps
genetic engineering
high-yield seeds
biotechnology
eutrophication
pesticide resistance
Mediterranean agriculture
specialized farm products
genetically modified organisms
  (GMOs)
animal welfare
natural food products
organic
dairying

milkshed
subsistence agriculture
extensive subsistence agriculture
monoculture, staple crop
multi-cropping
physiologic density
arable land
food preservation
specialized crops
subsistence farming
transhumance
cash-cropping
commercial crops
corporate agriculture,
  agribusiness
commodity chains
commodity prices
intensive agriculture: mixed
  farming, general farming
subsistence agriculture
market gardening
extensive agriculture
pastoralism
nomadic herding
slash and burn agriculture,
  swidden
shifting cultivation
fallow
plantation agriculture
domestic consumption
livestock ranching
human ecology
human-environment interactions
extensive pastoralism
population pressure
overgrazing
desertification
soil salinization
irrigation

Chapter 5 Key Terms

aquifers
deforestation
wetland
point sources
nonpoint sources
dead zones

point sources
nonpoint sources
dead zones
biomagnification
animal waste
mineral salts

CHAPTER 6

Industrialization and Economic Development

Now let's move from discussions of rural land use and farming to analysis of industrialization and its resulting economic development. Industrialization can transform the economic landscape for both the countries that it touches and the countries it does not touch, by creating tiers of nations—first world, second world, and so on. Let's dive into an exploration of development, manufacturing, and industrialization then in the next chapter we'll explore the venue where much of this happens—urban centers. In the words of CC Bloom in the cinematic classic *Beaches,* "oh, Industry."

Growth and Diffusion of Industrialization !

The rise of industrialization led to economic differences between states and countries—early growth and innovations align with early stage three in the Demographic Transition Model (see page 51). Technical innovations and migration movements in Europe and North America caused the rise and spread of industrialization in the 1800s and early 1900s. As work opportunities were eliminated in agriculture, manufacturing job opportunities increased in industrialized countries. However, these innovations took decades to reach the Third World. In this section we will discuss terms associated with the types of industrialized states and the factors that led to industrialization.

Levels of Economic Development !

We can categorize countries in terms of their level of economic development. We use the following terms to compare development level verbally and to acknowledge the patterns of **uneven development** in the world economy. Some categories are better descriptors than others and some countries aren't categorized as easily as others.

❶ **First World: Industrialized** and **service-based economies** that have free markets, a high level of productivity value per person and thus, a high quality of life. In addition to the United States and Canada, there are the European Union countries, Norway, Switzerland, Iceland, Israel, Australia, New Zealand, Japan, South Korea, Singapore, Taiwan, and Middle-Eastern oil states Saudi Arabia, Kuwait, United Arab Emirates, Oman, and Bahrain.

Borderline First-World economies might include Argentina, Chile, South Africa, and some island nations like Trinidad and the Seychelles. These have productivity statistics that are higher than the Third World, but not quite at First-World levels yet. You might be tempted to call them Second World, but that term has a very different meaning.

❷ **Second World:** Describes the **Communist** countries of which only two "hard line" Communist states remain today: Cuba and North Korea. These states still have centrally planned economies. The term is occasionally used to designate "former Communist" states that are still **restructuring** their economy to free-market systems like the former Soviet Union and Eastern European states, although many have joined the EU. It can also describe China and Vietnam, which are newly industrialized countries still controlled by Communist parties but that have adapted **free-market reforms** to their economies.

❸ **Third World:** Countries with mainly **agricultural** and **resource-based economies** that have low levels of per-person productivity and a low quality of life. These **underdeveloped states** are found across Latin America, the Caribbean, Africa, and the Asian countries not listed above. Some Third-World states have made a distinct economic shift toward industrialization and urbanization (see newly industrialized countries or NICs, below), while others remain firmly in a rural, agricultural category. Examples of the poorest Third-World states are Haiti, Niger, Malawi, Tanzania, Madagascar, Nepal, and the former USSR countries Kyrgyzstan and Tajikistan.

❹ **Fourth World:** Third-World states that have experienced some sort of **economic crisis** that has immobilized the national economy. Crises can include a crash of the country's banking system, devaluation of a country's currency, a failed government taxation system, or events that shut down the economy such as warfare and natural disasters.

❺ **Fifth World:** Third-World states that both lack a functioning economy (like Fourth-World states) and have no formal national government.

Emergence of Service Sectors ❗

Services are intangible products, as opposed to manufactured goods, which are physically tangible or touchable. As a group, services are the most valuable form of economic production. However, not all services are as valuable as others. One way to classify them is by the level of pay and benefits they provide employees.

Low-benefit services are sectors where the labor force tends to be hourly employees who receive few if any additional benefits, like paid vacation or health insurance. Examples of low-benefit service jobs include hotel and food services, retail, customer services, contract agricultural labor, and construction.

Conversely, **high-benefit services** are sectors in which pay tends to be salaried and includes considerable fringe benefits like health, dental, vision, vacation, sick days, and retirement reimbursements. High-benefit positions include the areas of business services, health care, government, and education.

The more common way to classify **service firms** is by the type of activity performed as part of the service:

Retailing   Labor and workforce

　　Food, travel, and tourism

　　　　　　Government

　　Education

　　　　　Transportation services

Environmental and waste management

　　　　　Construction and engineering

　　Energy utilities

Communication utilities

　　　　　Media and entertainment

　　Advertising and marketing

Medical, health, and personal care

Finance and banking

Insurance

Real estate

Accounting and business consulting

Legal services

Software, data, and computer consulting

Research and Development

Economies and the Demographic Transition Model ❗

The **Demographic Transition Model** has a number of uses. We touched on this model in Chapter 1, but will explore it in-depth here. By placing a country on this model, you are defining the **population dynamics** and **economic context** of that country. Knowing where a country falls on the model lets you know what kind of economy the country has, whether or not there is significant migration going on, and, like economic indicators, this "picture" of a country's population can tell you much about its quality of life. These are theoretical estimates and averages, and not all countries fit the model perfectly.

The model also provides insight into economic history. If we look at the United States, Canada, or Western Europe, we can apply dates to the bottom of the model to show how stage four countries have progressed through the system. Looking at the model on the next page, we can see in Western Europe the beginning of the Renaissance; in Western Europe and in the United States and Canada, the **Industrial Revolution;** and likewise the recent **deindustrialization** or shift to **service-based economies.** Pre-history goes all the way back to human beginnings. Fourteen hundred

---

 Economists like to joke that there are actually four types of national economies: developed countries, developing countries, Japan, and Argentina. This is because the last two have gone the opposite of the way of most economic trends.

represents the time when there was both a cultural and economic renaissance in Europe. Eighteen hundred represents the Industrial Revolution, when countries like the United States and Great Britain were **newly** industrialized countries (NICs). And 2000 represents a turning point of the rise of service-based economies of more developed countries (MDCs).

More Developed Countries & Less Developed Countries

More developed countries (MDCs) and **less developed countries (LDCs)** are terms used to describe the relative economic differences between states. First and Second World countries generally tend to fit in the MDC category, while Third, Fourth, and Fifth World are LDCs—even if they are NICs (Newly Industrialized Countries, which are discussed below). Where the dividing line is between the two categories is up to debate. If you are asked to assign MDC or LDC status to a country based on gross national product per capita or GNI PPP, use the following basic rule: $10,000 GNP per capita, above it are MDCs, below it, LDCs.

Newly Industrialized Countries

Newly industrialized countries (NICs) are Third World states that have economies that have made a distinct shift away from agriculture and toward manufacturing as the focus of economic development and production. Industrialization is a long-term process that can last decades in larger countries. NICs are in a constant process of building **infrastructure** (roads, ports, power plants, water systems, railways), which facilitate the construction and operation of factories.

Two characteristics of NICs link back to your knowledge of population and migration (back in Chapter 2). First, NICs have **rapid population growth** and are usually on the border of stage two and stage three of the demographic transition model. (Turn the page to see two of those.) Several more advanced NICs like Brazil, Mexico, and India are well into early stage three. China, due to its one-child policy, appears to be the most advanced in terms of demographic transition, but in fact it should be economically categorized with the other NICs. Secondly, NICs experience **rapid rural-to-urban migration** as their economies industrialize and, as a result, urbanize.

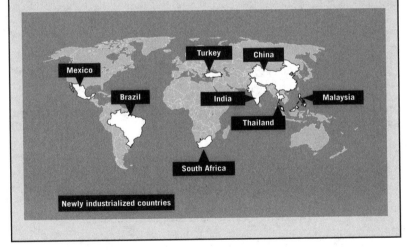

Newly industrialized countries

Demographic Transition Model

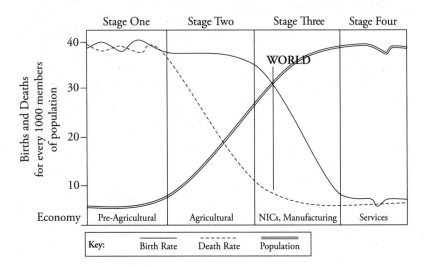

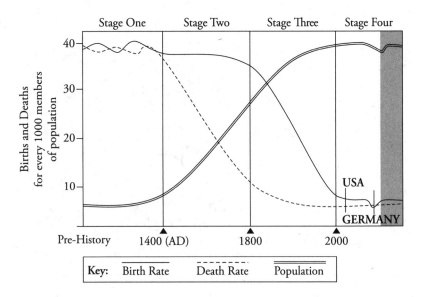

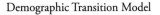

Identify Economic Sectors ❗

The economy can be divided into different categories known as **sectors.** What composes a sector of the economy can vary depending upon what is being categorized. One common way to group economic activity and employment is by its stage in the production process. This results in three to five categories. All the world's countries include each of these stages. Depending on a country's level of development, one sector will be more prevalent than the others.

Primary Production
- includes agriculture, mining, energy, forestry, and fisheries. These activities deal with the extraction of natural resources from the Earth.

Secondary Production
- includes the processing of the raw materials drawn from the primary sector. These activities and jobs also include the fabrication of components and the assembly of finished goods. In sum, secondary production reflects all forms of manufacturing. Other industries can include fisheries or service industries.

Tertiary Production
- includes the transportation, wholesaling, and retailing of finished goods to consumers. Tertiary production can include types of services that could be categorized as quaternary, like finance, or quinary, like government.

Quaternary Production
- includes wholesaling, finance, banking, insurance, real estate, advertising, and marketing. These are collectively called "business services."

Quinary Production
- includes retailing, tourism, entertainment, and communications, government, or semi-public services such as health, education, and utilities. These are known as "consumer services."

Role of Technology and Energy in Industrialization ❗

During the industrial era, the product that made all manufacturing possible was steel. Everything from railroad cars to skyscrapers and automobiles are made possible by steel alloys, as iron alone is too brittle and heavy. In the service economy era, the **computer** makes all sectors of the service economy more efficient and capable of handling large numbers of consumers and data. Even more specific is the impact of the **microchip,** as these miniature processor circuits have made desktop computers possible as well as smaller handheld and wireless devices.

Without technical innovations, industrialization would not have occurred, and the services industries in the First World today would not exist. Such innovations also necessitated alternative forms of energy. No longer could economies sustain themselves with simple, natural resources. The development of **mining** and **energy extraction** techniques led to new forms of energy and the trade of resources. Unfortunately, **resource-dependent countries** were, and sometimes still are, dependent upon trade from **resource-independent countries.** Such inequity of resources is directly connected to the economic development level of a country.

Measures of Social and Economic Development ❗

We use **economic indicators** to help understand the variable levels of development and measure the degrees of **uneven development** between states. In these figures, we can see the country-level economic differences created by gaps in development, technology gaps, and the poor standards of living created by the effects of colonialism, war, and disasters.

Gross Domestic Product (GDP) 🛈

GDP is the dollar value of all goods and services produced in a country in one year. It measures the total volume of a country's economy. This is done without adjusting for international trade; therefore it measures only the domestic economy:

$$GDP = GOODS + SERVICES$$

In addition, GDP is often reported in the news as "...quarterly GDP increasing by 3.5%..." This means that GDP for the most recent three-month quarter of the year grew by 3.5% over the previous three months (sometimes it's compared to the same quarter in the previous year).

Gross National Income (GNI) 🛈

GNI is the dollar value of all goods and services produced in a country, plus the dollar value of exports minus imports in the same year. It also measures economic volume. However, it adjusts for the "national" wealth lost when imported goods are purchased from abroad. And GNP includes wealth gained when money comes from other countries for exports:

$$GNI = GOODS + SERVICES + (EXPORTS - IMPORTS)$$

Many economists argue that GNI is a much more accurate measure of economic volume compared to GDP. In most countries, there is a foreign trade imbalance represented by either a positive or negative impact on the volume of the economy. In countries where export value exceeds import value, there is a **trade surplus,** which adds value to the economy. Conversely, in countries where import value exceeds export value there is a **trade deficit,** which removes value from the economy. Mathematically, this is what can happen:

- **Trade Surplus:** When EXPORTS > IMPORTS; adds value to economy.

- **Trade Deficit:** When EXPORTS < IMPORTS; removes value from economy.

The United States has a large trade deficit of nearly $502 billion caused by one significant imported good: oil. The volume of petroleum needed to fuel the U.S. economy and car culture requires the import of such a large amount of oil that it erases the value of American exports.

Per Capita Calculations 💬

To compare the level of development between countries, we have to use a *per capita* average. *Per capita* means in Latin literally "for every head," meaning for each person. Gross national income (GNI) *per capita* is the estimated income of a person converted to U.S. dollars at currency exchange rates. It is a modified form of GDP *per capita*. These **level of development comparisons** are done by dividing the volume of the economy by the population, like so:

GDP *per capita* = (GOODS + SERVICES) + POPULATION

GNI *per capita* = [(GOODS + SERVICES) + (EXPORTS − IMPORTS)] + POPULATION

These data are converted to U.S. dollars for comparison purposes. However, it's important to understand that these numbers are not indicators of personal income or the average salary of each worker. Instead, they are basically a measure of the country's collective wealth or productivity. It indicates a relative **standard of living** measured by the services that such productivity provides for the population.

The Gini Coefficient 〰

The **Gini coefficient** measures the level of **income disparity** between the country's richest and poorest population groups on a scale of 0 to 100, where 0 represents perfect equality and 1 represents total inequality. Higher numbers indicate a wide gap between the rich and poor and suggest major issues with poverty and the distribution of wealth in the country. Lower numbers indicate the existence of a large middle-class population where the nation's wealth is more equitably distributed. The graphs below illustrate the gini coefficient.

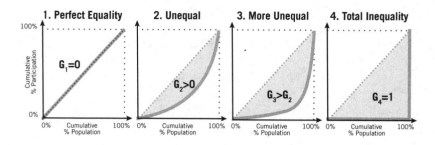

| 1. Perfect Equality | 2. Unequal | 3. More Unequal | 4. Total Inequality |

$G_1 = 0$ $G_2 > 0$ $G_3 > G_2$ $G_4 = 1$

Total Fertility Rate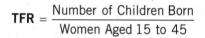

By definition, the **total fertility rate (TFR)** is the estimated average number of children born to each female of birthing age (15 to 45). TFR can be calculated as follows:

$$\text{TFR} = \frac{\text{Number of Children Born}}{\text{Women Aged 15 to 45}}$$

However, the TFR *is not an annual statistic* like the RNI. It is more of an estimate, taken as a snapshot of fertility for birth over the prior 30 years. Thus, TFR and RNI are not comparable. They are two different things—apples and oranges. You cannot have a negative TFR, for one thing. TFR highlights the importance of population replacement.

The Birth Rate 😎

Natality, which is the **crude birth rate (CBR)** or just the birth rate, as we will call it here, is an annual statistic. The total number of infants born living is counted for one calendar year and then calculated.

$$CBR = \frac{\text{Number of Live Births}}{\text{Total Population}} \times 1{,}000$$

High birth rates (18 to 50) are found in mostly rural agricultural Third-World countries and low birth rates (8 to 17) are more likely to be found in urbanized industrial and service-based economies. However, without knowing what's going on with mortality in that country (death rate), it's hard to know whether the population is growing and how quickly.

The Death Rate 😎

The mortality rate, also known as the **crude death rate (CDR)** or what we'll simply call the death rate, is an annual statistic calculated in the same way. The number of deaths are counted for the calendar year in a country and divided by every thousand members of the population

$$CDR = \frac{\text{Number of Deaths}}{\text{Total Population}} \times 1{,}000$$

Historically, higher death rates and **infant mortality rates** were recorded in the poorest of Third-World countries where the combination of poverty, poor nutrition, epidemic disease, and a lack of medical care resulted in low **life expectancy.** However, as conditions have improved in the Third World through the **Green Revolution** (increased food and nutrition) and access to sanitation, education, and health care have increased, life expectancies have gone up, and the death rate has gone down.

 Having Deja Vu?

If this birth rate and death rate stuff sounds familiar, it is! We looked at these items in Chapter 2, just in a different context. Can't hurt to plug it in here again—a lot of topics in AP Human Geography are connected in myriad ways.

Spatial Patterns of Economic Development

Rostow's Stages of Growth

Another approach to understanding the development process was developed in the 1950s by theorist Walt Rostow, who later became national security adviser to President Lyndon Johnson. Rostow proposed that countries went through five stages of growth between agricultural and service-based economies. One of Rostow's assumptions was that each country had at least some form of **comparative advantage** that could be utilized in international trade and thus fund the country's economic development over time. The five stages progressed as follows:

1. Traditional Society

The economy is focused on primary production such as agriculture and fishing. The country's limited wealth is spent internally on things that do not promote economic development. Technical knowledge is low.

2. Preconditions for Takeoff

The country's leadership begins to invest the country's wealth in infrastructure such as roads, ports, electrification, and school systems that promote economic development and trade relations with other nations. More technical knowledge is learned that stimulates the economy.

Industrialization and Economic Development

3. Takeoff

The economy begins to shift focus onto a limited number of industrial exports. Much of the country still participates in traditional agriculture, but the labor force begins to shift to factory work. Technical experience is gained in industrial production and business management.

4. Drive to Maturity

Technical advancements diffuse throughout the country. Advancements in industrial production are seen in many sectors of the economy, which grows rapidly. Workers become increasingly skilled and educated, and fewer people are engaged in traditional activities like agriculture.

5. Age of Mass Consumption

An industrial trade economy develops where highly specialized production such as vehicles, energy, and consumer products dominate the economy. Technical knowledge and education levels are high. Agriculture is mechanized and employs a small labor force.

Criticisms of Rostow's Stages of Growth 🗨

Rostow's model is based on the historical development patterns of the United States and other industrialized countries. Although the model provides a framework for the economic development of nations, not all countries have had the capacity to utilize potential comparative advantages for international trade. For example, colonial powers extracted many of the valuable natural resources in the Third World. When these colonies gained independence, they had limited or zero access to the wealth that had been extracted from their countries during the colonial era, and many of the resources that existed within their borders were technically owned by multinational corporations.

The **colonial legacy** and other barriers to development such as **government corruption** or **capital flight** (see the dependency theory, below) are not accounted for in Rostow's theory. He assumed that all countries could progress smoothly through the stages if their investment focused on trade and technology development. Realistically, the world economy tends to leave many countries far behind, as the large sums of international investment needed to develop an industrial economy tend to be focused only on the most capable and stable newly industrialized countries (NICs).

Wallerstein's World Systems Theory 🔔

Developed by Immanuel Wallerstein, the **world systems theory** suggests that there exists a world economic system that benefits some and exploits others. Wallerstein espoused that there are three types of countries: core, periphery, semi-periphery.

Core countries are capitalist countries that are economically and militarily powerful and not dependent on a single state or country. Core countries tend to exploit peripheral countries for raw materials and labor, a tendency that continually reinforces the inequity between the two. The United States is an example of a core country.

Conversely, **periphery countries,** commonly referred to as Third-World countries, do not have a strong central government, are dependent upon core countries for capital, and have underdeveloped industry. Cape Verde, an archipelago off of Africa, is an example of a periphery country. Check out the diagram below that might look like a chart of how circles with arms hug one another, but actually illustrates Wallerstein's World Systems Theory Model.

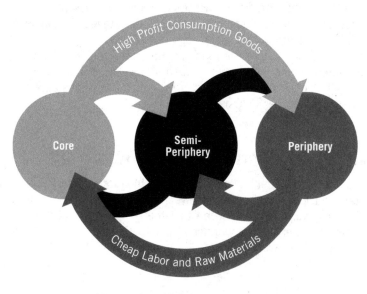

Wallerstein's World Systems Theory Model

Semi-periphery countries share qualities of both core and periphery countries; generally, these countries are either declining core countries or ascending periphery countries. India is an example of a semi-periphery country.

Dependency Theory ❗

Dependency theory holds that most LDCs (including all NICs) are highly dependent on foreign-owned factories, foreign direct investment, and technology from MDCs to provide employment opportunities and infrastructure. The main problem arises when Third-World countries get stuck in a continuous **cycle of dependency** on First-World loans to pay for additional economic development needs.

These concerns were first raised in Argentina in 1950 by economist Raúl Prebisch. The **Prebisch thesis** detailed the dependency of Third-World economies on First-World loans and investments to pay for the building of new industries and infrastructure. At the heart of Prebisch's theory stands a claim about the dominant role of First-World–based **transnational corporations** (TNCs) and investors in a postcolonial exploitation of the Third World in which MDCs have economically and politically subordinated LDC populations. Some describe this as **economic imperialism** in a modern reference to the European empires of the colonial era.

Industrialization Location Theory ❗

The location of factories has been the focus of much economic and geographic study. Going back to the work of **Alfred Weber,** whose 1909 *Theory of Industrial Location* is still influential, the selection of optimal factory locations has much to do with the minimization of land, labor, resource, and transportation costs. Weber states that in terms of location, manufactured goods can be classified into two categories based on the amount of inputs in relation to product output: weight-losing or weight-gaining manufacturing. This should sound familiar, as we discussed this back in Chapter 1. Flip back to page 11 for a quick refresher on that.

An added issue for food products such as bread is the limited shelf life that also affects industrial location. Bread, milk, and other **perishable products** tend to be manufactured in many individual plants that serve the local regions. This **decentralized network** approach keeps fresh products in stores longer by reducing transportation time. Bread production is so decentralized that bakeries are found in all cities and are an example of **ubiquitous industries.** Conversely, when shelf life is not an issue for weight-gaining manufacturing, production tends to be centralized within larger consumer market areas. Frozen foods, for example, are made in large centralized facilities, which then ship to stores and grocery warehouses across the country.

Transformation of the Contemporary Economic Landscape 🔊

Site and situation can still be used today to compare the economic prominence of cities. Economic site factors such as land, labor, and capital can be used to estimate the capacity of industry and services to develop in a particular place. Competition between cities for new business locations and new jobs are intense. How much land is developed, how educated the workforce is, and how much investment capital is available in a city are important indicators of the potential for urban economic development. There are a number of economic development approaches that you should be familiar with for the AP Human Geography exam.

Agglomerations and Growth Poles 💬

When things are grouped together on the Earth's surface, it is referred to as a **cluster.** When clustering occurs purposefully around a central point or an economic **growth pole,** it is referred to as **agglomeration.** In heavily populated areas, competition within markets is common. Also, planning and zoning rules often push some types of businesses with similar building space requirements into the same local areas. In the case of manufacturers and corporate services, firms will often locate near one another in search of technical knowledge and labor sharing. Economic **multiplier effects** around these centers have resulted in a multitude of companies and investment in computer hardware and software development. Consider the following examples.

- Computer hardware and software firms in the **Silicon Valley** area south of San Francisco: This is due to close proximity to the high-tech **growth poles** of Stanford University and the NASA Ames Research Center.

- Automobile companies in **Detroit:** This was originally due to manufacturing cost **advantages** of location on the Great Lakes for iron ore delivery by water, and proximity to coal in the Midwest and Appalachia.

- Banks in **South Dakota:** The state of South Dakota has **limited banking regulations** and no corporate taxes. Some national banks have facilities where large corporate and institutional accounts are held to avoid the high auditing costs and banking profit taxes of other states.

Comparative Advantage vs. Complementary Advantage 〜

The term **comparative advantage** means that a party has the ability or resources to produce a good or service at less cost and more efficiently than other states. As such these advantageous goods and services are selected for industrial production over other possible alternatives.	Conversely, the term **complementary advantage** means that parties have a comparative advantage over complementary areas of production. In turn, these countries partner to benefit both economies.

Free-Trade Zones !

Regional free-trade agreements between states have become a common way to improve international trade. Remember our discussion of supranationalism back in Chapter 4? Supranational **free-trade zones** like the European Union (EU) and North American Free Trade Agreement (NAFTA) have made regional economies of multiple states much stronger and have opened the doors of development for less developed neighbors. In the case of the EU, new member states that were once part of the Soviet Union or former Communist states in Eastern Europe have been able to develop their free-market economies more quickly.

Free-Market Reforms 💬

In the 1980s, Communist states like China and Vietnam began to reform the old soviet-style **command economy** in which all economic production was managed and planned by the central government. These reforms included allowing farmers to sell surplus agricultural goods in local and regional markets for profit. In cities, the reforms allowed people to open privately owned businesses like restaurants, repair services, and transportation companies. Other reforms such as the free movement of labor and the ability to purchase private real estate have also been introduced.

The most significant reform is allowing foreign companies to open factories and retail services in these countries. China established the first **special economic zones (SEZs)** in 1980, in which foreign firms were allowed to build facilities in coastal port cities. SEZs are a type of **export processing zone,** defined as port locations where foreign firms are given special tax privileges to incentivize trade. China's SEZs were such a success that by the late 1990s, all of the coastal provinces in China and Vietnam had been opened to foreign manufacturing firms. Low-cost labor, land, and utilities provided by provincial governments were in large demand by transnational corporations seeking to maximize factory profits, which are shared with the Chinese and Vietnamese governments.

Industrial and Manufacturing Zones ❗

In addition to knowing the aforementioned types of industrial zones, make sure to know the location and composition of the major industrial regions around the world:

North America
American Industrial Belt or "Rust Belt" following deindustrialization
Canadian Industrial Heartland or Canada's "Main Street"
Piedmont Industrial Region

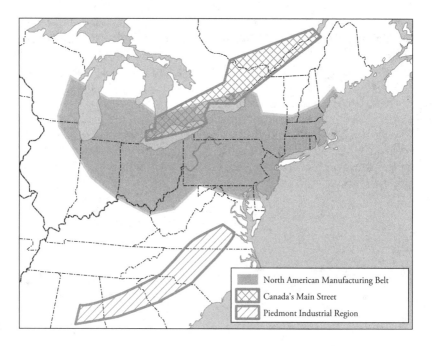

 Bob Seger Fans: Don't Be Confused. Bob Seger is a proud Detroit native, but his song "Main Street" is NOT about Canada's Main Street, as shown in the map above.

ASAP Human Geography

Europe

British Midlands
Ruhr Valley
Northern Italy or the "Third Italy"

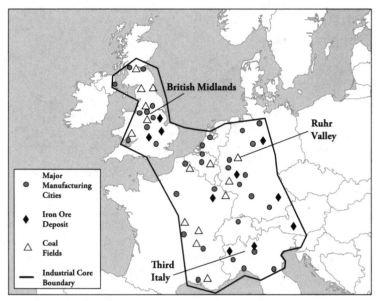

European Industrial Core

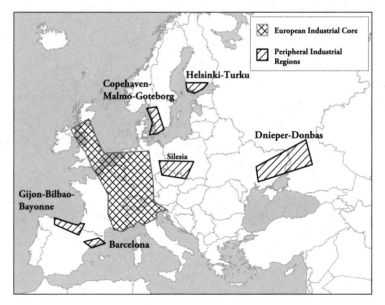

Asia
Japan, Korea, Taiwan, and China

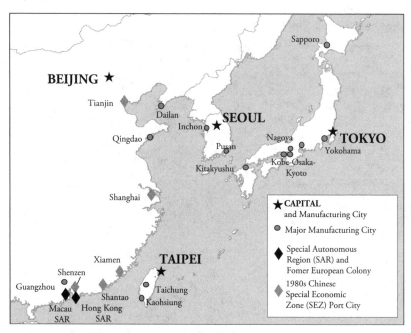

Other World Industrial Regions

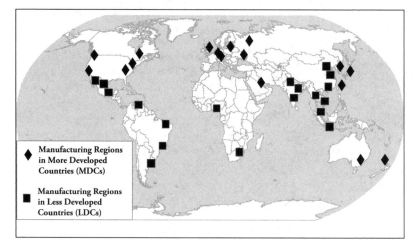

Deindustrialization ❗

When we analyze the overall economic productivity of First-World countries such as the United States and Canada, it soon becomes clear that services produce the majority of the countries' economic value and employment. In recent history the United States and Canada, like other service-based economies, have **deindustrialized,** shifting away from manufacturing as the main source of economic production.

The downside is that in the 1970s and 1980s when deindustrialization was widespread in Anglo-America and Western Europe, millions of factory workers lost jobs and many old industrial cities suffered from the economic downturn. The workforce had to adjust to new service sector employment that paid less and had fewer benefits compared to unionized factory jobs. Manufacturing businesses also had to focus on highly priced manufactured goods like vehicles, heavy equipment, and computing devices to keep profits and investment up amid **foreign competition** and keep the remaining First-World manufacturing labor force paid and employed.

Sustainable Economic Development ❗

Products drawn from living resources like fisheries and forestry are renewable. Our ability to continuously rely on a resource depends on the **sustainable use** of the resource. This means that fish cannot be taken from the sea in amounts that they cannot replace themselves (with or without the help of hatcheries). Likewise, forest replanting is necessary for trees to be available perpetually. How trees are cut and how fish are caught makes a difference in terms of overall **ecosystem** survival and sustainability.

Natural Resources ❗

Natural resource production can be divided into two pairs of linked sectors based on their renewability and prices: mining and energy extraction and fisheries and timber markets.

1.

Mining and **energy extraction** can be valuable depending on the global commodity prices. Oil export-based economies such as Saudi Arabia and Venezuela can rise and crash with the radical price changes. Such price volatility is difficult for both producers and consumers. Likewise, copper-mining countries like Zambia are doing well now that metal prices are rising. However, this **resource-dependent country** was economically devastated in the early 1980s when one of the largest consumers of copper, the U.S. Mint, decided to switch to cheaper zinc cores for pennies—a move that caused a global crash in the price of copper.

2.

Fisheries and **timber markets** are not as volatile, but have increased in price and value over the years due to reduced supply. However, in these heavily regulated and increasingly protected natural resources, companies must use more technology and larger processing facilities to remain profitable and meet growing consumer demand, especially from large and growing newly industrialized markets such as China and India.

Renewability 🔔

We can also classify resources by their renewability. Minerals and fossil fuel energy are **nonrenewable products.** Once they are extracted, the earth cannot reproduce them. Energy sources that do not run on fossil fuels are generally **renewable** if managed properly. With the exception of hydroelectricity, **alternative energy** sources such as solar, wind, nuclear, tidal, and geothermal power tend to be more expensive to harness than fossil fuels and are thus less common. Despite this history, technological advances continue to bring down the cost of renewable energy to bring it closer to parity with nonrenewable energy.

 Did You Know?

On April 30, 2017, 85% of the electricity consumed by Germany was generated by renewable sources.

Environmental Effects of Development 🔔

Environmental pollution is a detrimental effect of industrialization. Excessive use of agricultural chemicals can poison soils and water supplies. In addition, improper usage of pesticides could lead to birth defects in children, forcing parents to move to cities to seek constant medical care for their children. Natural disasters can also work as push factors. A flood or drought can destroy a whole year's income and cause people to leave farming as their primary source of income.

Consider China. Industrial development in China and the newly earned wealth of the Chinese people have combined to create a large demand for energy in industry and transportation. Coal has been the primary source for electrical production and is plentiful in the country. Oil demand is also high, as industry and Chinese citizens have more use for truck and personal cars. China is not oil-rich and has invested heavily in oil exploration and production in the Third World, including in politically sensitive countries such as Sudan and Myanmar. The other problems faced by the Chinese are pollution in the form of urban smog, acid rain, and an increasingly large portion of the world's greenhouse gas emissions.

Chapter 6 Key Terms

more developed countries (MDC)
less developed countries (LDC)
newly industrialized countries (NIC)
infrastructure
rapid population growth
rapid rural-to-urban migration
computer
mircochip
mining
energy extraction
resource-dependent countries
resource-independent countries
Alfred Weber
Theory of Industrial Location
perishable products
decentralized network
ubiquitous industries
sectors
economic indicators
uneven development
Gross Domestic Product (GDP)
Gross National Income (GNI)
trade surplus
trade deficit
per capita
level of development comparisons
standard of living
The Gini Coefficient
income disparity
total fertility rate (TFR)
crude birth rate (CBR)
crude death rate (CDR)
infant mortality rates
life expectancy
Green Revolution

Rostow's Stages of Growth
comparative advantage
colonial legacy
government corruption
capital flight
world systems theory: core, periphery, semi-periphery
dependency theory
cycle of dependency
Prebish thesis
Transnational corporations
Economic imperialism
uneven development
First World
Second World
Third World
Fourth World
Fifth World
Demographic Transition Model
population dynamics
economic context
Industrial Revolution
deindustrialization
service-based economies
low-benefit services
high-benefit services
service firms
cluster
growth pole
agglomeration
multiplier effects
cluster
growth pole, agglomeration
multiplier effects
comparative advantage
complementary advantage

Chapter 6 Key Terms

free-trade zones
command economy
special economic zones (SEZs)
export processing zone
deindustrialized
foreign competition
sustainable use

ecosystem
mining, energy extraction
fisheries
timber markets
nonrenewable products
renewable
alternative energy

CHAPTER 7

Cities and Urban Land Use

Why do settlements or cities form where they do? In this chapter, we'll think back to when the cities we know today were just settlements. This section will review the spatial concepts related to central place theory and discuss why cities are located in a particular place and how they become prominent places among the mass of other similar settlements. We'll explore factors that influence urbanization and suburbanization, different types of cities and their respective structures, and urban planning and design. Buckle up, city slickers!

Urban Settlements ❗

Urban Origins

Where do cities or settlements come from? The origins of an urban place often have to do with one of two categorical factors:

1. Access to resources—towns and cities of this type are called **resource nodes**. An example of this would be Lowell, Massachusetts, during the Industrial Revolution, when jobs in factories were plentiful so tons of people (mostly women) relocated to Lowell for work, and built a bustling city.

2. Access to transportation—towns and cities of this type are called **transport nodes.**

British new towns have been revitalized through access to transportation. For example, the British town of Runcorn has dedicated busways enclosed by housing. Similarly, many suburbs surrounding major cities cropped up thanks to transporation (large scale highways, trains, bus routes) from the city center out to more sprawling areas where housing was built.

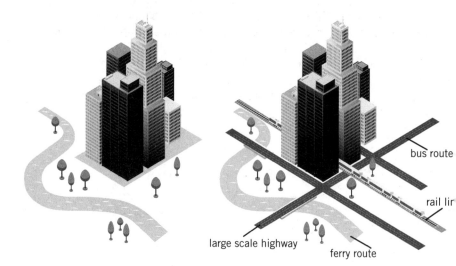

bus route

rail lir

large scale highway

ferry route

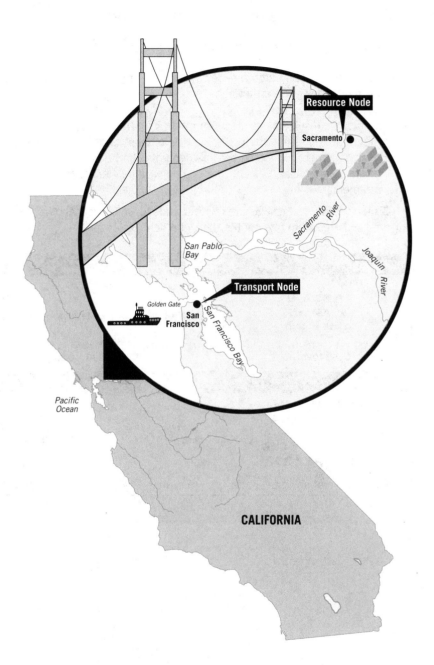

Settlement Patterns ❗

Patterns of rural settlements are described by the relative location of their residential and farm structures.

- **Clustered rural settlements** are communities in which all of the residential and farm structures of multiple households are arranged closely together. Some clustered settlements can be further classified as **circular** or **linear**, depending on the shape of the settlement.

- **Dispersed rural settlements** are communities in which households are separated from one another by significant distances.

Clustered	Linear Clustered
Close together	Close together along a road or stream front
Circular Clustered	**Dispersed**
Close circle around open space	Separated by significant distances

Factors that Influence the Origin, Function, and Growth of Cities

Familiarize yourself with these factors that influence cities:

- **Site** describes the physical characteristics of a place or its absolute location.

- **Situation** describes a place's relationship with other locations, or its relative location.

- **Threshold** is the minimum number of people required to support a business in the city.

- **Range** is the maximum distance people are willing to travel to gain access to a service from the city.

SITE: Why this spot?
SITUATION: What else is around?
THRESHOLD: Are there enough people for business?
RANGE: How far away is everything else?

New York City became the most prominent trade and finance center in the United States during the 1800s. So what's the big deal about NYC?

GOOD SITE:
- Large, deep water harbor
- Next to Atlantic Ocean

NEW YORK

Boston
Philadelphia
Charleston

GOOD SITUATION:
- Hudson River for easy trade
- Centrally located among other cities on eastern seaboard
- Major port on Atlantic Circular Trade Route

 Sorry, Boston, Philadelphia, Charleston, but when it comes to trade and finance circa 1800, New York City's good site and good situation made it the most prominent trade and finance center of the United States.

Borchert's Epochs of Urban Growth ❗

University of Minnesota geographer John R. Borchert created a model that expresses five distinct periods of American urbanization and the impact of transport technology developments and changes on the epoch. Those epochs are:

Epoch's name	Time period	Information
Sail-Wagon Epoch	1790–1830	Cities crop up near ports and major waterways, as those are the dominant modes of transportation.
Iron Horse Epoch	1830–1870	This era is about the development and impact of steam engine technology, steamboats, regional railroads.
Steel Rail Epoch	1870–1920	Come on ride the train (and ride it)—this time is all about the development of long haul railroads and the growh of a national railroad network.
Auto-Air-Amenity Epoch	1920–1970	This epoch is characterized by the gasoline combustion engine and the modes of transport technology that emerged from that.
High-Technology Epoch	1970–Present	This epoch is about the development and expansion of service and information technology sectors.

The transition between these periods were complex; among other factors, the westward expansion of the United States helped to press the need for innovations. Borchert established these periods by examining cities based on size order.

Evolution of the Modern City

1790–1830	1830–1870	1870–1920	1920–1970	1970–Present
Sail-Wagon Epoch	Iron Horse Epoch	Steel Rail Epoch	Auto-Air-Amenity Epoch	High-Technology Epoch

Ask Yourself...

In this chapter, we are exploring how the modern city evolved over the years thanks to technological development—in what ways do we see that same type of development in agricultural and rural changes? Can you draw any parallels between advancement in urban life and advancements in rural life?

Global Cities and Megacities ❗

A **megacity** is a metropolitan area with more than 10 million people. Don't memorize the list but know a few examples:

Rank	City	Population (in Millions)
1	Tokyo	37.8
2	Delhi	25.0
3	Shanghai	23.0
4	Mexico City	20.8
5	São Paulo	20.8
6	Mumbai	20.7
7	Osaka	20.1
8	Beijing	19.5
9	New York City	18.6
10	Cairo	18.4

United Nations World Urbanization Prospects 2014

Now let's take a look at the pros and cons of life in a big city. And what better way to start this, than with a Hollywood movie-style poster?

Challenges Experienced ❗

Big cities have their pros and cons. They have gobs of culture, activities, jobs, and opportunities, not to mention a wide assortment of people, but they also face their share of assorted challenges and difficulties. Let's explore a few of the different types of challenes that cities face.

Economic Challenges

- Infrastructure requirements to attract business
- Utilities, transportation, safety, health, and education needs must be met
- Escalating costs of living and salary expectations due to desire for rare commodities and inflated real estate prices

Agglomeration

We've heard of this term before, but let's review just to be sure it's totally clear—**agglomeration** is when similar business activities are found in a local cluster. Sometimes this happens becaue of zoning laws, sometimes it's because certain labor pools are found in an area, sometimes it's corporate strategy. Ever notice that a popular drug store opens across the street from another one? Believe it or not, this configuration has advantages for the businesses and consumers alike. For example, did you know that Starbucks often opens franchises directly across the street from one another so that drivers don't have to make a left-hand turn?

Social Challenges

Big cities can experience major social challenges exacerbated by the wide assortment of types of people living within their borders and the ongoing influx of new people into a big city. The issue of invasion versus success comes up a lot in cities—the long-term turnover of a neighborhood's social and ethnic composition.

Here are a few of the major social challenges of urban existence that you should be familiar with:

- **Segregation:** Segregation is illegal in the U.S. (thanks to the Civil Rights Act of 1964), nonetheless many urban areas are divided up along racial and cultural lines. For example, Chinatowns were historically areas where Chinese, Filipino, and Japanese immigrants were forced to live. Nowadays, many cities have their own little Chinatowns and while some urban residents are thrilled that the Chinese culture is being preserved and passed down, others feel that retaining culture in this way causes tension and isolation.

- **Redlining:** Neighborhoods on company maps where home mortgage and insurance applications are automatically denied based on the demographics of those areas. These institutionalized systems keep lower classes from advancing and keep these neighborhoods in disrepair, as would-be small business owners simply couldn't secure loans to build businesses there.

- **Restrictive covenants:** Areas in which homeowners add special covenants to their home real estate titles which restrict future sale of a home to white-only buyers.

- **Racially steered districts:** Districts where real estate companies purposefully drive non-whites to racially specific neighborhoods, regardless of their income.

Environmental Challenges

To close out this depressing section with even more downer facts, here's a list of the assorted environmental issues inherent in urban development: traffic congestion, smog, greenhouse gases. Can we talk about something remotely uplifting now, please?

Models of Urban Systems ❗

Check out this handy chart that helps explain distribution size of cities:

What'cha Call It?	What's It Do?
Rank-Size Rule	A country's second-largest city is half the size of its largest, third-largest city is one-third the size of its largest,...nth largest is 1/n size of its largest. We covered this in an earlier chapter, so you may be having déjà vu, but that's a good thing!
Law of the Primate City	Largest city has at least twice the population of the next largest; negative impact could be urban primacy which causes imbalance in the country.
Christaller's Central Place Theory	Seven levels of places—from small hamlet to large regional serve-center city—that follow a regular pattern (again, déjà vu?).

To Explain Interactions Among Networks of Cities ❗

Gravity Model

This model is used to calculate transportation flow between two points, determine the area of influence of a city's businesses, and estimate the flow of migrants to a particular place.

$$\frac{Location_1 \; Population \times Location_2 \; Population}{Distance^2}$$

To Explain Internal Structures of Cities & Urban Development ❗

The downtown or city center area of a city is called the Central Business District (CBD). This area is usually the peak land value intersection (PLVI), which is the area within a settlement with the greatest land value and commerce. It's usually found in the CBD and has an assortment of transport links (roads, rail options). Nowadays, a lot of cities are revitalizing their **Industrial zones**, spots that were originally sites of industry, and are now becoming reborn as parks, museums, sports stadiums, arenas, convention centers, outdoor concert venues. The High Line park in the Meatpacking District of New York City is a perfect example of this.

You have probably heard of suburbs—housing settlements just outside the city where families can buy single-family houses with a bit of space but can still easily commute into the urban center. But have you ever heard of exurbs? (It has nothing to do with your ex-boyfriend or ex-girlfriend—fear not.) Exurbs are large tracts of land owned by wealthy people, including suitcase farmers who both work in the city and keep farms out in the country.

Now it's time for our favorite spin-off from *America's Next Top Model,*
AP Human Geography's Favorite Urban Models:

Name	Summary	Visual
Burgess Concentric-Zone Model	As working class moves toward center for work, higher classes move out and commute.	
Hoyt Sector Model	Working class surrounds transporatation line, higher classes begin in town center and radiate out.	
Harris-Ullman Multiple-Nuclei Model	Although city began around the CBD, other, smaller CBDs sprouted in the outskirts of the city, creating multiple business foci, or nuclei.	

Ask Yourself...

Are you fascinated by these descriptions of urban models and good
versus bad urban planning? If so, head to your local library or favorite
bookstore and get a copy of *The Death and Life of Great American
Cities* by writer and activist Jane Jacobs.

To Explain Internal Structures & Urban Development in Metropolitan Areas ❶

Galactic City Model

In the last half of the twentieth century, urban geographers have noticed that many of the new suburban Central Business Districts in the U.S. and Canada have become specialized and geared toward a particular industry or sector. This Galactic City Model represents a distinct decentralization of the commercial urban landscape as the economy has transitioned to services as the leading form of production. Manufacturing hasn't disappeared—it has just declined significantly and become specialized. That specialization has meant that new manufacturing facilities tend to be smaller and less expensive than they used to be.

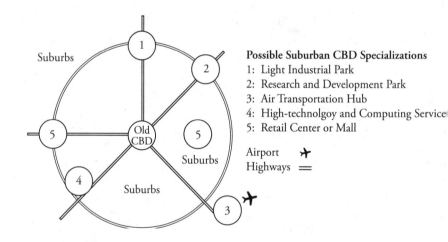

Possible Suburban CBD Specializations
1: Light Industrial Park
2: Research and Development Park
3: Air Transportation Hub
4: High-technolgoy and Computing Service
5: Retail Center or Mall

Airport ✈
Highways ═

To Explain Land Use and Urban Development

The model we just mentioned is designed only to represent North America; other countries are different and only only one of these appears regularly on the AP Human Geography Exam. Fortunately, you already read about it so you are ahead of the game! Flip back to Chapter 1 and review these models:

Latin America

- von Thünen Model (see page 8 for diagram).
- Weber Model (see page 11).

African City Model

This model has 3 central business districts: colonial (leftovers from the colonial CBD), traditional CBD, and a market zone. On the outermost part of the cities, residents make their home anywhere (these are shantytowns, poor neighborhoods). The image expresses this clearly:

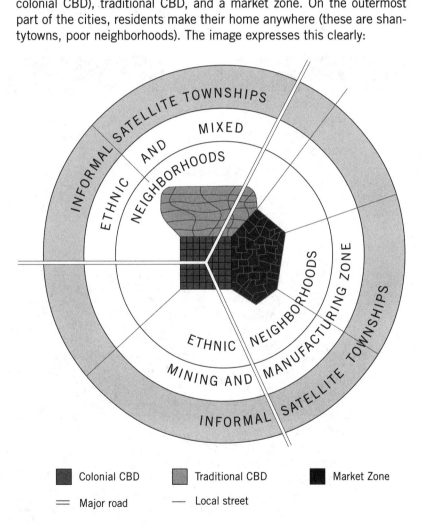

■ Colonial CBD	■ Traditional CBD	■ Market Zone
═ Major road	— Local street	

Built Environment and Social Space 🔔

Residential Land Use

Residential land use is just that—land used for residences (family homes of any type) and there are 3 ways it can be split up:

Type of Housing	What Does That Mean?	Example
Low	Low-density housing means that isn't a lot of density—that is, there aren't a lot of people around. So low density housing would be, for example, single family homes on large lots of land where you may have an acre or more between you and your nearest neighbor (ideal for loud parties).	
Medium	Medium-density housing is a bit more crowded—examples of this include single-family homes on smaller lots (perhaps your neighbors are pretty close to you—you can chat over the fence) or townhouses/condominiums.	
High	High-density housing means there's a whole lotta people around. Examples of this include high rise apartment buildings, condominiums, or anywhere that you find a lot of people living per square foot.	

Evaluate Infrastructure of Cities ❗

To remain viable, liveable, desirable, and financially solvent, cities have certain infrastructure requirements. Economic growth in cities tends to occur only in urban areas where utilities, transportation, safety, health, and education needs are met in terms of access and capacity.

Cities that attract new service firms must have centers that promote financial growth. This occurs when the centers have access to sound: (1) public transportation, (2) airports, (3) roads, (4) communication systems, (5) water/sewer systems.

Urban Planning and Design ❗

Sustainable Design Initiatives

A current trend in urban planning and design is the emergency of sustainable design, which is the philosophy of designing physical objects, buildings, and homes to comply with the principles of economics, social, ecological sustainability.

One type of urban planned development that falls under the umbrella of "sustainable design initiatives" is the walkable mixed-use commercial and residential areas. A "mixed use" development is a type of urban development that combines residential, commercial, cultural, industrial uses, and more, to create a hub where all of those parts are completely integrated and the average resident can walk around (a car isn't required). Sustainable designs are bolstered by what are called **Smart-Growth Policies**—policies of development that promote a mix of building types and uses (mixed use, baby!), diverse housing and transportation options, encourage community engagement, preserve open space and natural beauty, and create walkable neighborhoods where engaged community members can live and work. A few examples of Smart-Growth Policies include:

- **New Urbanism**—mixed-use developments that implement buildings which contain both housing and commercial space
- **Green Belts**—bands of largely undeveloped, wild, or agricultural land surrounding or neighboring urban areas.

- **Slow-Growth Cities**—decrease the rate at which the city grows horizontally to avoid sprawl and its adverse effects

But urban planning and design isn't always done well and good intentions don't guarantee positive results. We'll be closing out this book on a bit of a downer note and discussing the problems associated with the growth of urban areas.

Problems & Solutions Associated with Growth and Decline of Urban Areas ❗

Unfortunately, there are myriad problems associated with the growth and decline of urban areas. You may see some of these buzz words when you read about these items in the newspaper currently, so some may look familiar. Look through these items and know that you may see them again on the AP Human Geography Exam, so perhaps keep some current day examples in mind.

- **Housing Discrimination**—Housing discrimination is a pervasive problem nationally and is severely under-reported, because often victims of housing discrimination don't even know that they are being discriminated against. Federal law prohibits housing discrimination based on your race, color, national origin, religion, sex, familial status, or disability, but some academics compare housing discrimination to modern-day segregation.

- **Housing Affordability**—Urban areas, with their public transportation and assortment of restaurants, stores, industries, (that is, potential jobs) often appeal to less affluent people. When wealthy people come to the cities and, for example, "flip" apartments or homes (buy, renovate, resell at a huge mark-up), they price out these urban dwellers who cannot afford the new housing prices.

- **Access to Public Services**—After World War II, when home owner-ship began to boom (thanks to federal home loan programs such as the G.I Bill), many people began leaving cities and heading out to sprawling homes in newly developed suburbs. This boom in suburban home construction prompted a number of service providers (family doctor, grocer, auto mechanic, gift shops) to relocate from cities out to the subrubs. Companies brought their services to where the suburban consumers lived—effectively moving the CBD (central business district) from the cities out to the suburbs.

- **Gentrification**—This is a buzz word that you may hear on the local and national news. Due to real estate prices dropping after industrialization, urban dwellings were purchased at low prices and redeveloped (in many cases, flipped as we mentioned above).

- **Sanitation**—Any crowded overpopulation creates sanitary conditions that are difficult to control, so sanitation can be a source of difficulty in growing urban areas.

- **Air Quality**—A large number of cars in a small area is a significant source of (1) smog which is harmful to public health and creates an unsightly haze; and (2) greenhouse gases that contribute to global warming. On the bright side, many U.S. cities have adopted bike share programs and bike trails in an attempt to encourage urban dwellers to use modes of transporation that aren't cars.

 Ask Yourself...

Have you read about the concept of "food deserts" in the newspaper recently? How might that phenomenon be connected to the issues that we are discussing here? How much you introduce those concepts in an AP Human Geography essay?

Chapter 7 Key Terms

resource nodes
transport nodes
clustered rural settlements—
  circular, linear
dispersed rural settlements
site
situation
threshold
range
Borchert's Epochs of Urban
  Growth: Sail-Wagon, Iron Horse,
  Steel Rail, Auto-Air-Amenity,
  High-Technology
megacity
agglomeration
growth poles
segregation
redlining

restrictive covenants
racially steered districts
Rank-Size Rule
Law of the Primate City
Christaller's Central Place Theory
gravity model
industrial zones
Burgess Concentric-Zone Model
Hoyt Sector Model
Harris-Ullman Multiple-Nuclei
  Model
Galactic City Model
Smart-Growth Policies
New Urbanism
Green Belts
Slow-Growth Cities
housing discrimination
housing affordability

NOTES

NOTES

NOTES

NOTES

NOTES

NOTES

International Offices Listing

China (Beijing)
1501 Building A,
Disanji Creative Zone,
No.66 West Section of North 4th Ring Road Beijing
Tel: +86-10-62684481/2/3
Email: tprkor01@chol.com
Website: www.tprbeijing.com

China (Shanghai)
1010 Kaixuan Road
Building B, 5/F
Changning District, Shanghai, China 200052
Sara Beattie, Owner: Email: sbeattie@sarabeattie.com
Tel: +86-21-5108-2798
Fax: +86-21-6386-1039
Website: www.princetonreviewshanghai.com

Hong Kong
5th Floor, Yardley Commercial Building
1-6 Connaught Road West, Sheung Wan, Hong Kong
(MTR Exit C)
Sara Beattie, Owner: Email: sbeattie@sarabeattie.com
Tel: +852-2507-9380
Fax: +852-2827-4630
Website: www.princetonreviewhk.com

India (Mumbai)
Score Plus Academy
Office No.15, Fifth Floor
Manek Mahal 90
Veer Nariman Road
Next to Hotel Ambassador
Churchgate, Mumbai 400020
Maharashtra, India
Ritu Kalwani: Email: director@score-plus.com
Tel: + 91 22 22846801 / 39 / 41
Website: www.score-plus.com

India (New Delhi)
South Extension
K-16, Upper Ground Floor
South Extension Part-1,
New Delhi-110049
Aradhana Mahna: aradhana@manyagroup.com
Monisha Banerjee: monisha@manyagroup.com
Ruchi Tomar: ruchi.tomar@manyagroup.com
Rishi Josan: Rishi.josan@manyagroup.com
Vishal Goswamy: vishal.goswamy@manyagroup.com
Tel: +91-11-64501603/ 4, +91-11-65028379
Website: www.manyagroup.com

Lebanon
463 Bliss Street
AlFarra Building - 2nd floor
Ras Beirut
Beirut, Lebanon
Hassan Coudsi: Email: hassan.coudsi@review.com
Tel: +961-1-367-688
Website: www.princetonreviewlebanon.com

Korea
945-25 Young Shin Building
25 Daechi-Dong, Kangnam-gu
Seoul, Korea 135-280
Yong-Hoon Lee: Email: TPRKor01@chollian.net
In-Woo Kim: Email: iwkim@tpr.co.kr
Tel: + 82-2-554-7762
Fax: +82-2-453-9466
Website: www.tpr.co.kr

Kuwait
ScorePlus Learning Center
Salmiyah Block 3, Street 2 Building 14
Post Box: 559, Zip 1306, Safat, Kuwait
Email: infokuwait@score-plus.com
Tel: +965-25-75-48-02 / 8
Fax: +965-25-75-46-02
Website: www.scorepluseducation.com

Malaysia
Sara Beattie MDC Sdn Bhd
Suites 18E & 18F
18th Floor
Gurney Tower, Persiaran Gurney
Penang, Malaysia
Email: tprkl.my@sarabeattie.com
Sara Beattie, Owner: Email: sbeattie@sarabeattie.com
Tel: +604-2104 333
Fax: +604-2104 330
Website: www.princetonreviewKL.com

Mexico
TPR México
Guanajuato No. 242 Piso 1 Interior 1
Col. Roma Norte
México D.F., C.P.06700
registro@princetonreviewmexico.com
Tel: +52-55-5255-4495
+52-55-5255-4440
+52-55-5255-4442
Website: www.princetonreviewmexico.com

Qatar
Score Plus
Office No: 1A, Al Kuwari (Damas)
Building near Merweb Hotel, Al Saad
Post Box: 2408, Doha, Qatar
Email: infoqatar@score-plus.com
Tel: +974 44 36 8580, +974 526 5032
Fax: +974 44 13 1995
Website: www.scorepluseducation.com

Taiwan
The Princeton Review Taiwan
2F, 169 Zhong Xiao East Road, Section 4
Taipei, Taiwan 10690
Lisa Bartle (Owner): lbartle@princetonreview.com.tw
Tel: +886-2-2751-1293
Fax: +886-2-2776-3201
Website: www.PrincetonReview.com.tw

Thailand
The Princeton Review Thailand
Sathorn Nakorn Tower, 28th floor
100 North Sathorn Road
Bangkok, Thailand 10500
Thavida Bijayendrayodhin (Chairman)
Email: thavida@princetonreviewthailand.com
Mitsara Bijayendrayodhin (Managing Director)
Email: mitsara@princetonreviewthailand.com
Tel: +662-636-6770
Fax: +662-636-6776
Website: www.princetonreviewthailand.com

Turkey
Yeni Sülün Sokak No. 28
Levent, Istanbul, 34330, Turkey
Nuri Ozgur: nuri@tprturkey.com
Rona Ozgur: rona@tprturkey.com
Iren Ozgur: iren@tprturkey.com
Tel: +90-212-324-4747
Fax: +90-212-324-3347
Website: www.tprturkey.com

UAE
Emirates Score Plus
Office No: 506, Fifth Floor
Sultan Business Center
Near Lamcy Plaza, 21 Oud Metha Road
Post Box: 44098, Dubai
United Arab Emirates
Hukumat Kalwani: skoreplus@gmail.com
Ritu Kalwani: director@score-plus.com
Email: info@score-plus.com
Tel: +971-4-334-0004
Fax: +971-4-334-0222
Website: www.princetonreviewuae.com

Our International Partners

The Princeton Review also runs courses with a variety of
partners in Africa, Asia, Europe, and South America.

Georgia
LEAF American-Georgian Education Center
www.leaf.ge

Mongolia
English Academy of Mongolia
www.nyescm.org

Nigeria
The Know Place
www.knowplace.com.ng

Panama
Academia Interamericana de Panama
http://aip.edu.pa/

Switzerland
Institut Le Rosey
http://www.rosey.ch/

All other inquiries, please email us at
internationalsupport@review.com